Sheldon,

As a fellow entrep.

who writes of many oth

crazy but beautiful entrepre urs,

I'm confident these stories

and characters will

resonate with you.

Enjoy!

Kurt

PRAISE FOR *WHO'S YOUR MIKE?*

"Who's Your Mike? *has it all—crazy entrepreneurs and loyal, hardworking and overwhelmed employees. This book hit home for me and helped me navigate my way with my growing business. Kurt speaks my language and shows the reality of the pitfalls we face in an unapologetic way."*

– Molly Hunt
CEO of Ty Boyd, Inc.

"Founders who are scaling their companies successfully eventually find that they have too much 'start-up culture' in their organization, which can be painful for the team to endure. There comes a day when we have to face the reality that we're lacking executives who can build and scale processes. Who's Your Mike? *will provide some clarity on this subject for entrepreneurs everywhere."*

– Paul Hedrick
Founder & CEO of Tecovas

"Kurt Wilkin doesn't have much patience for business books. Mostly because he finds they tend to be 80 percent fluff. (I came to the same conclusion covering entrepreneurs for Inc., Forbes, *and* The New York Times.*) A true entrepreneur who has built several successful professional service firms, Kurt has seen the inner workings of countless businesses. As a result, he has written a book for impatient entrepreneurs like him—filled with real stories and only the stuff that matters. It's about the art of hiring, firing, and developing people. And given the current labor climate, it could not be better timed."*

– Loren Feldman
Editor-in-Chief of *21 Hats*

"This book was meant for people exactly like me. I recently spoke with an entrepreneur friend who is going through something akin to what I was experiencing, and I thought of 'Mike'! It really helped to know that many entrepreneurs go through similar challenges. The loneliness I was feeling lifted after reading the first few chapters."

– **Amy Sweet**
CEO of Halcyon Home

"As a leader you can be so close to your people it can be hard to see things clearly. Who's Your Mike? *provides great perspective and helps bring things into focus."*

– **Kevin Ainsworth**
Founding Partner of GuideCap Partners

"These insights really hit home and brought back some tough memories! I just wish I had the opportunity to read this book before having to deal with my own Mike!"

– **Christi Chatmas**
Co-Founder and CEO of Caddie Central

"Kurt draws you in with real-life stories that resonate. Whether you're an entrepreneur or looking to take that plunge, this is a must-read!"

– **Brett Lawson**
Founder and CEO of The CFO Suite

"The stories Kurt shares in Who's Your Mike? *are eerily familiar. I've seen so many of these characters in my career, and entrepreneurs everywhere will recognize most of them, as well. For most entrepreneurs, there comes a time when you realize you've simply outgrown key members of your team."*

– **Doug Tatum**
Author of *No Man's Land*

"Kurt nailed it! Every character in Who's Your Mike? *worked in my startup. Each story really resonated with my real-world experience and I appreciated all the sage advice!"*

– Carl Natenstedt
Serial Entrepreneur, Founder, CEO of Z5 Inventory

"Kurt is uniquely positioned to share stories that are raw and real based on his lived experiences working with entrepreneurs. He shares his scar tissue and wise insight that you can both relate to and practically apply."

– Jacquie Hart
Global CEO Coach, Partner, and Chief Connector of CEO Coaching International

"Today, there is a war on talent. Are you winning or losing? Who's Your Mike? *is written for entrepreneurs who employ people. The relatable characters and stories in this book will help you with your own employee challenges and ensure you win the war on talent."*

– Erik Qualman
5X #1 Bestselling Author and Professor

"Entrepreneurs often look for a silver bullet when it comes to hiring. Who's Your Mike? *will dispel that myth and provide pages of powerful stories, tips, and tools for dealing with the 'people' part of growing your company."*

– Rand Stagen
CEO of Stagen Leadership Academy

"With these 'so true it hurts' stories, Kurt brings his real and down-to-earth style to life in Who's Your Mike?! *Very real accounts of the people-problems we all face as leaders, most that we bring on*

ourselves by growing our companies! Save yourself tons of heartache and time by learning from this book. I wish I had this guide when I launched my company!"

– **Jonathan Ulrich**
Owner, CEO, and Visionary of Ulrich Barn Builders

"We all know that to be successful, we need to have the right players in the right seats, but making that happen is where the magic exists. Who's Your Mike? *will help you find that magic (and avoid repeating mistakes along the way)!"*

– **Ramona Cappello**
Serial Entrepreneur and Partner at CEO Coaching International

"Who's Your Mike? *is an important guidebook for entrepreneurs who have hired friends and family. As we grow our companies, we need to grow our teams, and setting 'Mike' free can be a challenge. Kurt's book helps you address your 'Mike' so your company can grow and, ultimately, 'Mike' can too!"*

– **Kathleen Quinn Votaw**
TalenTrust Founder and author of *Dare to Care*

WHO'S YOUR MIKE?

A **No-Bullsh*t** Guide to the People
You'll Meet on Your Entrepreneurial Journey

KURT WILKIN

Published in association with Per Capita Publishing, a division of Content Capital®.

Although the author and publisher have made every effort to ensure that the information in this book was correct at press time, the author and publisher do not assume and hereby disclaim any liability to any party for any loss, damage, or disruption caused by errors or omissions, whether such errors or omissions result from negligence, accident, or any other cause.

ISBN 13: 978-1-954020-24-5 (Paperback)
ISBN 13: 978-1-954020-28-3 (Hardback)
ISBN 13: 978-1-954020-25-2 (Ebook)

Library of Congress Cataloging-in-Publication Data
Names: Wilkin, Kurt, author.
Title: Who's Your Mike? / Kurt Wilkin
Description: First Edition | Texas: Per Capita Publishing (2022)
Identifiers: LCCN 2022902163 (print)

First Edition

WARNING: The characters described in the pages that follow may induce anxiety, night sweats, and panicked calls to your executive coach or advisor. Some will seem all too familiar. There could be one right down the hall. You may even think you're reading about yourself at some point. But don't be alarmed: Each chapter will provide tips and advice for navigating your way out of this personnel nightmare. Unless otherwise indicated, the names, businesses, places, and stories in this book have been anonymized in order to protect the innocent. If you see your story in the book—congratulations, send the author a note. If you see yourself in any of the characters . . . you might be the problem.

To my parents: Dad, you taught us the power of storytelling and many entrepreneurial lessons from the School of Hard Knocks! Mom, you taught us grace . . . and to never give up.

To my wife and three boys: Carrie, thank you for having faith in me . . . in good times and in bad. Luke, Brady, and Bennett, thank you for keeping me humble!

To entrepreneurs everywhere: Here's to the struggles, the sleepless nights, the gray hairs, and the frugal beginnings. I hope and pray it will all be worthwhile someday.

TABLE OF CONTENTS

PREFACE

WHO'S YOUR MIKE?

As entrepreneurs we're always looking for the silver bullet. An easy fix for the challenges that inevitably come our way. I have a feeling that's why most of us pick up business books in the first place.

Unfortunately, life doesn't come with silver bullets.

My name is Kurt and I invite you to join me in a conversation about people. Specifically, the types of employees you'll likely encounter on your entrepreneurial journey. Because, as we all know but rarely understand, your company is only as strong as your people.

I've worked with high-growth companies for almost thirty years. I've made a boatload of mistakes myself and I've witnessed exponentially more. And many of those came from having the right people in the wrong seat and vice versa. I had to learn my lessons the hard way. My hope is that you can learn from these mistakes so you can avoid them yourself—with this book as your guide.

My Problems with the "Traditional" Business Book

Like many entrepreneurs, I've got a stack of business books on my nightstand—most of which I simply can't get through, if I'm being honest. Sure, there're a few I've read cover to cover because I found them to be engaging, informative—and yes—entertaining. Books like *The Five Dysfunctions of a Team* by Patrick Lencioni, *Start with Why* by Simon Sinek and *Good to Great* by Jim Collins should be on everyone's list of must-read business books. And in my references I've listed a bunch of other books which have shaped my thinking as an entrepreneur—and advisor to fellow entrepreneurs.

However, while the vast majority of business books may have a few pearls of wisdom, most just don't have enough to carry me through an entire book. Believe me—I've tried! I've had a ton recommended to me, and I've purchased most of them! I would bet that, on average, you really only need to read 20 percent of each of the "amazing" business books you've been recommended. The problem is, you just don't know *which* 20 percent!

I also think most of them are simply too fluffy. They're written by successful leaders or consultants who tell you how great you'll be if you just follow "my ten-step process" or "my eleven keys to business success." As such, there are too many stories of rainbows and unicorns, and not enough straight talk about everything that can, and inevitably does, go wrong.

If you're anything like me, you learn by example. Either directly through your own pain and suffering, or from the stories of others. Real-life stories. Personally, I want to learn from your challenges and successes and apply them to my situation. And don't just give me glory stories, I want the gory stories. The messier the better. The bigger the shit show, the more powerful the lesson!

The Importance of Talent

We all know the importance of a strong team. We need to get the "right people on the bus" (Jim Collins in *Good to Great*) and get the "right people doing the right thing right" (Verne Harnish in *Mastering the Rockefeller Habits*), and some of us have explored the EOS® Right People Right Seats exercise (from Gino Wickman's *Traction*).[1]

Based on my two-and-a-half decades working with entrepreneurs, I can confirm that most of you know you need to recruit great people to build a great business. But it's just as important, if not more, that you put those great people in the right roles—and get rid of poor performers and bad apples. Sounds easy enough, right? Like most things in business, the seemingly easy stuff is often the hardest—especially for entrepreneurs who are eternal optimists, or hate having challenging conversations, or just want everyone to "do their f-ing job and leave me alone!"

That's why I'm writing this book. I want to start a conversation about all aspects of talent. And I want the leaders of entrepreneurial companies to relate to the real-life stories within. No pie in the sky. My hope is that you can connect these stories with your own and make the changes needed to take your business to the proverbial next level. Some of these stories are mine, and others have been gleaned from the hundreds of business leaders

I've worked with in my eleven years at HireBetter and my previous sixteen years in professional services. I'm here to help you learn from my observations and my own very real challenges.

The best part? You don't even have to read the entire book! Just read the chapters that speak to you. Take what you want and ignore the rest. This way I can stay true to my nobody-reads-an-entire-business-book-because-they're-80-percent-bullshit mantra! But I have a sneaking suspicion you'll find a lot more than 20 percent will apply to you.

About This Book

We've all made hiring mistakes. It's simply impossible to get every hire right. Sure, there are tools you can use to minimize the risk of making a mistake; the marketplace is riddled with assessments or psychometric tests like Predictive Index, TTI Success Insights, and DISC, as well as hiring practices like Topgrading and HireVue. There are thousands of recruiting firms who claim to be able to help you hire "the best" or "the fastest" or "the cheapest" talent. And, of course, there are reputable recruiting firms like Spencer Stuart and Egon Zehnder; and recruiting partners like HireBetter. But it's impossible to bat 1.000 on new hires.

The bottom line is that you're going to make mistakes. No matter what system you use, no matter what recruiters you bring in, and no matter how much you pay for assessments or the flavor-of-the-month recruiting tool, everyone makes hiring mistakes. This book will help you reduce your hiring mistakes on the front-end and will help you validate (or invalidate) your thinking when you believe you've made one.

How about employees in the wrong seats? Yep, we have those too. We all do! Every entrepreneur has someone on their team who: (a) they've outgrown; (b) is in the wrong seat; (c) was a great individual contributor but crappy leader or manager when promoted; (d) has simply become a problem-child; or (e) fill in the blank. They're just not a good fit in their current role.

By the end of the book, you'll be able to spot the bad ones from a mile away when recruiting. And you'll be able to identify people you need to move into other seats—or simply remove them from the damn bus. My hope is that you'll learn a few tips about how to avoid certain situations and how to have productive conversations when the time comes.

This book isn't just about hiring better and firing better, it's about helping you decide who you need to hire, who you need to invest in, who needs to be reassigned, and who needs to go—yesterday. All high-growth, entrepreneurial companies have employees they've simply outgrown, even key ones. I've seen it many times—yesterday's hero is today's liability. Many of us promote long-term employees into leadership roles only to realize we made a mistake, and they need to be moved back into an individual contributor role.

I hope you identify with some of these stories and they help you see solutions you may not have seen before. Trust me, no one has all the answers and there's no secret formula. Anyone who tells you otherwise . . . is simply full of crap.

Lastly, keep in mind that ***this*** book focuses on challenges with your employees and recruiting and hiring for your organization. We recognize that sometimes the challenges begin (and often end) with the entrepreneur . . . but that's a whole 'nother story.

INTRODUCTION TO

WHO'S YOUR MIKE?

At the time of this publication, the number-one thing keeping the leaders of entrepreneurial companies awake at night—is talent. Access to great talent. Recruiting and retaining A-players gets most of the attention. There's a second challenge that isn't talked about as much: employees with whom we need to part ways, whether by firing them, counseling them out, or helping them find another job. But a third one is RARELY, if ever, discussed, despite the fact that it causes a ton of headaches. I'm talking about the long-term, legacy employee whose role has outgrown his or her capabilities. Yesterday's hero who has turned into today's headache.

This is a real problem for companies that are growing and scaling. In fact, it's so common that everyone with whom I share the following story has seen it in their own companies. Every time I tell it, heads nod vigorously, and founders and CEOs lament their own situations, past or present.

I've seen variations of this story hundreds of times—with practically every client, colleague, or peer—and even in my own companies. I firmly believe that if you're honest about your own situation, you'll recognize this employee in your midst. In fact, I'm so confident that, once you've read this story, if you can honestly tell me you haven't seen this situation yourself, drop me a line and I'll buy you a taco and a beer the next time you're in Austin!

Meet Mike

Mike was your fraternity brother in college, your best friend. You would do anything for each other, and you did a decent job of keeping each other out of trouble and surviving school. Mike has a marketing degree, but he did take three hours of accounting. He thinks he got a B in the course, but honestly, he barely remembers going to class.

A few years after college, you started your business in your garage and Mike was right there with you, nights and weekends. He seemed to understand numbers and you trusted him with your life, so he became your go-to guy for all the accounting and administrative crap you don't fully get. He taught himself QuickBooks and turned himself into a helluva part-time bookkeeper.

As your fledgling startup went from "great idea" to "let's f-ing do this!" Mike was there every step of the way. Your baby became a real company, and it didn't take much to convince Mike to quit his crappy 9-to-5 job to work with you.

Mike's official title was accountant. He was in charge

of keeping the books, making sure your three other employees and your vendors got paid accurately and in a timely manner. But in reality, Mike was your right-hand man. He did anything and everything you asked him to—and more. Need some numbers crunched, some dirty work done, or floors swept? Mike was there. No questions asked.

Over time, the company grew and became more and more legitimate. You added other key employees to your team, but Mike was always there by your side. Real companies need real titles, so Mike was promoted to controller. For him, it was the next logical title, it looked great on a business card, and he earned it with his dependability and work ethic. You trusted Mike implicitly and there was no one you'd rather have in the foxhole with you.

Now, your company is growing like crazy! It looks like you timed the market perfectly—customers love your product. As the company expanded in every way, so did Mike's responsibilities. You decided to promote him to CFO because you wanted the bank to stop bothering you and talk to him! It was the next logical step for him anyway, and he was your most senior accounting and finance person (actually, he was the ONLY one in that department). More importantly, Mike asked for the title, and he was busting his ass, so you looked at this as a way to reward him. And titles sure are cheap for early-stage companies!

Five years in, and you guys are crushing it. You're now pushing $20 million in revenue and Mike's right there, with his three hours of accounting and QuickBooks certification under his belt. Mike's working 100-hour weeks to keep up. He's essentially learning on the job—and he hasn't learned to delegate, so he's basically doing the job of three accountants.

Bigger companies lead to bigger opportunities—and bigger challenges. In addition to his day job, Mike is attempting to negotiate a $10 million line of credit with the bank, while simultaneously negotiating the acquisition of one of your biggest competitors.

But Mike isn't a true CFO. He's overwhelmed, overworked, and, well, he's in way over his head. You know Mike is working hard, but you don't know the full extent. In addition to his 100-hour weeks, Mike hasn't taken a vacation in years and he's struggling mightily to keep all the balls in the air. Mike doesn't want to let you down. So you don't know all the implications . . . until it's too late.

Mike has become a bottleneck—a damn good one. He's extremely loyal to you and he wants so badly to be your go-to guy, but things are falling through the cracks. The bubblegum and duct tape that was holding everything together begins to give way. Mike has never had the skills or experience to manage all of these next-level CFO responsibilities, no matter how hard-working, loyal, or trustworthy he is.

It's taking longer and longer for him to get the books closed and financial statements out. In fact, you're losing confidence in his numbers, and he's struggling to track down facts and figures for leadership meetings. You're having to hound him for basic details, and now you've found yourself covering for him. And Mike, your good friend and key lieutenant, is utterly, wholly exhausted.

Who's *Your* Mike?

Maybe your Mike isn't in accounting and finance. Maybe he's in sales, operations, or product development. But trust me—you have one! In all my years as an entrepreneur and working with hundreds of other entrepreneurs, this was right up there with death and taxes: one of the few certainties in business. I've had Mikes on my own teams and I'm confident that you have, have had, or will have, your very own Mike.

Telling a Story

I used to ask clients if they had someone on their team that the company had outgrown—their own Mike. And I'd usually get an immediate, defensive "NO" for an answer. After all, no one wants to admit that yesterday's hero, yesterday's trusted lieutenant, perhaps even your best friend, is now a liability to the organization in their current role. But when I told them my "Who's Your Mike?" story, it hit home.

Let's face it, the best way to learn is the School of Hard Knocks. I'm a prime example. I learn my most valuable lessons the hard way—by getting knocked on my ass! But I also found out that I learn pretty well by hearing the stories of others—kind of an entrepreneurial cheat code.

I know I'm not the only one. Many of us (especially entrepreneurs) seem to learn better through hearing the nitty-gritty, real-life stories of others. (Definitely better than reading a damn run-of-the-mill business book, that's for sure!) Personally, I don't have patience for your "12 Steps to a Better Team" or your workbook on how to hire effectively. Enough with the business book gobbledygook. Tell me your story and it will stick with me. And, as I said before, the bigger the shit show, the better my retention of what to do—or better yet, what not to do!

That's why I'm writing this book. My hope is that you can relate these employee-centric stories to your own situation and make the changes needed to take your business to the next level. In this book you'll meet many of the characters I've witnessed on my own journey, like Mike. You'll meet senior-level "leaders" brought in from the outside, like Pipeline Paul, Techno Tim, and Resume Ralph. And you'll read about legacy employees like Right-Hand Rita, Bounce-Around Betty, and Harry the Hustler. Some are lost causes, some have outgrown their original role, and some can be triaged. But they're not all bad. In fact, some might thrive in a new role with the right guidance, coaching, and support.

A number of these stories are mine—and others I've gleaned from the hundreds of business leaders I've worked with over more than twenty-seven years in professional services. I've taken a lot of notes along the way, and I'm here to help you learn from these very real challenges.

So, What Do I Do about Mike?

I'm confident that after reading about the characters in this book, taking a fresh look at your own people issues, and reading the suggestions in the Intermission chapters, you'll come away with the clarity and confidence to handle your own Mike (or Paul or Tim or Betty) situation.

So, buckle up! You're about to enter the chaotic world of the entrepreneur. You'll get an up-close look at many of the characters those guys and gals encounter as they slog their way through the entrepreneurial phases of growth in order to successfully grow their companies. Enjoy!

> Think you have a Mike? Or a Paul, Rhoda, Harry, or Tim? Take my free assessment at Who'sYourMike.com/quiz and take the first step toward identifying your people challenges and opportunities.

01

WHAT ABOUT MIKE?

YOUR BOOKKEEPER-TURNED-CFO

"Most rapid growth companies stagnate when they reach a certain point and outgrow legacy employees. They need experienced hires who have done this before, who have already made the natural mistakes that are part of the learning process. Mistakes made on other people's dimes."

– **Doug Tatum,** *No Man's Land*

Remember Mike? The do-everything lieutenant when you started your company in your garage, who became your CFO as you barreled toward $20 million in revenue? Funny thing is, he didn't seem so overtitled until recently; now he seems to be overwhelmed on a daily basis.

You might find you're more and more frustrated with Mike these days . . . but is it possible that you set him up for failure? He excelled when your team was full of generalists who did a little bit of anything and everything, so you rewarded him with titles and responsibility. He still works his tail off, but he's simply unable to make the jump to kickass CFO.

So, what do you do with Mike? He's been by your side from the beginning, and he's been incredibly loyal, someone you could count on. Do you simply accept the new reality of fast-growth mode—that he's going to make a ton of mistakes as he learns lessons the hard way—inevitably stunting your company's growth in the process? Do you move him into an individual contributor role and bring in a more experienced person to lead the team? Do you make the hard choice to let him go?

I bet this sounds familiar. I've seen some version of this play out with virtually every entrepreneurial client, friend, or peer I know. Your Mike may not be in accounting and finance. He or she might be in sales, operations, or product development. But you have (or have had) one: someone who has been by your side for much of your journey, loyal and willing to do almost anything that's asked. They've been rewarded with promotions and responsibilities to the point where their titles are inflated and they're so far over their heads that they're at risk of imploding. And they're utterly exhausted.

So, let's figure out what to do with your Mike.

What's Wrong with Mike?

It's one thing to recognize you have a Mike and acknowledge that he's holding you and your company back. It's another thing altogether to take the hard steps to do something about it!

As you scale your business, there are steps you need to take in order to professionalize it. One of the main things holding your Mike back is often one of the reasons he was so great early on. He's a bootstrapper who isn't afraid to roll up his sleeves. He won't ask his team to do anything he won't do. But that's the thing—he never built a team. He struggles with delegation and tends to do things himself. He says things like, "I'll just do it myself. It'll take longer to teach someone else how to do it." Truth be told, this is a common struggle for many entrepreneurs too—myself included.

As we dive into other personalities throughout the book, we'll talk about solid performers who lack the drive and initiative to grow and take on challenges. Maybe they're B-players. But Mike is the opposite. He's willing to go the extra mile and work 100-hour weeks for you and the company. This character trait is vital for startups, but it often doesn't work as well at the next level—where you need to work smarter, not harder.

Mike simply isn't the guy for the job at the next-level, at least not *yet*. But it's not for lack of trying. He's just not a true leader. He's always done everything himself, and he definitely doesn't know how to identify, recruit, and onboard game-changing talent—people who are more talented than he is! These traits weren't necessary when he was employee number three in a five-person company. But now that you're scaling your organization, you need a different skill set.

Celebrate Mike

Let's take a step back and appreciate what it means to have a Mike on your team. While it's a new challenge, it also means you're crushing it! You're building a badass company. You started from zero and you're well on your way. Congratulations! You should be proud of what you're building. Consider Mike to be a badge of honor—you've grown past the point where you're relying on the herculean efforts of a few.

You're not alone. As I've said before, we all have someone on our legacy team that we've simply outgrown. As much as we hate to admit it, very few team members are going to make it from zero to $100 million with you. But guess what? That's OK! Some people are *great* at, are built for, and enjoy the startup phase. Some are better at improving what's already there and growing from $20 to $100 million. And some are built for companies several hundred million dollars and beyond.

> It's important to recognize that not everyone on your team will be able to (or want to) evolve and grow with the company as it grows from a wet-behind-the-ears startup to a Fortune 100 behemoth. And that's OK.

Exposing Mike

Sometimes it's hard to recognize—or admit—that you have a Mike. I know. I've been in your shoes, and I've worked with hundreds of entrepreneurs who have as well.

This is especially hard because Mike has been there for you over the years, managing all of those back-office functions that are absolutely necessary but make you crazy just thinking of them. Thank God for Mike. He's bought himself some well-deserved grace for what he's meant to you.

As the company grows, you're willing to overlook some red flags, turn a blind eye to deficiencies, and make excuses: "Mike's exhausted. Why isn't his team able to step up and help him?" or "Mike's working his tail off, but the financials are late again, and they're wrong again." or "We need a workaround, so we don't have to wait on Mike."

If you've ever said anything like this about one of your "key" employees—that's probably your Mike. And if you're not sure, I included some simple but effective questions at the end of this chapter and in Intermission I on page 81 to help you figure it out.

Yesterday's hero is today's liability. The "superhero" method doesn't work long-term. Leveraging his heroic efforts used to work, but it simply doesn't scale. I realize this is tough. You wouldn't be where you are without him, but you can't get where you need to with him doing everything—especially when those things aren't done well!

The Opportunity Lost

Look, it's not that Mike couldn't eventually figure things out, but having Mike in the wrong seat will slow you down and you'll learn a lot of lessons the hard way. Simply put, you'll better amplify your growth with the right people in the right seats. Allow me to illustrate the difference by sharing two stories about a homegrown entrepreneurial superstar (and good friend of mine).

> **Hard knocks:** Kraig was a classic bootstrapping entrepreneur. He founded Kraig's Kombucha in college with his grandfather's recipe and a $10,000 loan. He brewed kombucha in his parents' kitchen for the first two years of existence and sold bottles out of the back of his Volkswagen van at music festivals and parks across Texas.
>
> As a bootstrapper like many of you, he did things the old-fashioned way: rolling up his sleeves, working 100 hours a week, hiring cousins, neighbors, friends of friends, and doing whatever it took to survive. Not only did he survive, but over the next eleven years, his business grew to $15 million in annual revenue. Solid growth, but boy, was it a slog!
>
> He attracted a private equity partner who invested some growth capital and assessed his team. They quickly saw gaps on Kraig's team, including the finance function. They helped him transition his "Mike" to an indi-

vidual contributor role in accounting, where he was well-suited. They then brought on a finance leader and a head of operations who had successfully navigated explosive growth for similar beverage companies, and they were on their way. Kraig's growth was exponential, and within a few years, the company was acquired by a strategic buyer for $183 million. Quite a success story!

Version 2.0: Fast-forward a few years and Kraig was at it again. He leveraged his beverage experience and founded a tequila company around the same time I co-founded HireBetter. On a Young Presidents Organization (YPO) trip, I shared with him my rationale behind HireBetter and how I wanted to be a Strategic Talent Partner versus a "traditional" recruiting firm. He said, "Kurt, I get it. I've seen the light. I've seen what happens when you hire people who've done it before to replace the start-up generalists. This time I want to do that much earlier than last time. I want to buy their experiences, I want to buy their Rolodexes."

So he did. With SoCo Tequila, we helped him upgrade his operations "Mike" early on, and Kraig outsourced his finance and accounting function until it made sense to hire an A-player CFO on a full-time basis. Throughout the organization, Kraig repeatedly hired next-level talent ahead of the curve, and even replaced himself as CEO in year two.

The results were electric. SoCo Tequila grew rapidly—reaching that same $15 million mark in just three years. A prime example of how bringing in experienced next-level talent can help entrepreneurial companies amplify their growth—reaching their goals faster and with fewer lessons learned the hard way. SoCo made a powerful case study after three years, but it gets better. Just eighteen months later, the company was sold to a strategic buyer for a whopping $450 million!

I love this story because it not only highlights the importance of identifying your own Mikes and hiring next-level talent, but it's also a great example of the opportunities lost when you struggle with a team full of Mikes!

A Real-Life Mike

My friend Kate is the CEO of a B2B software and services firm in Texas. The company was growing very rapidly and was around $5 million in software-as-a-service (SaaS) revenue when she hired her first true accountant, Michelle. Michelle was a godsend for Kate during the next five years. She managed the company's cash with an iron fist, personally overseeing every single purchase. And she was meticulous with every line item in the financial statements.

In addition, she took on almost every administrative duty in the company. She managed the office lease, ordered furniture, negotiated with the electric company, and probably even took out the trash. She acted as HR manager, selected the payroll provider, oversaw the health insurance renewal process, managed payroll, and approved vacation requests. She pretty much managed everything for the back office so Kate wouldn't have to!

But the company started experiencing significant growing pains as it approached $25 million in annual revenue. Michelle's title was now CFO, and she controlled the purse strings. Everything that required money ran through her, which wasn't necessarily a good thing. The iron fist I mentioned earlier had become a death grip—because she was a CHEAPSKATE! A few examples:

- She wouldn't let the team compensate new hires for more than the bottom quartile, based on salary surveys for similar positions in Texas. As a result, they weren't able to attract the best and brightest talent and had significant turnover.
- She refused to let the team (including Kate, the CEO!) hire any administrative support. Her explanation? "They can do their own administrative work—I do my own!" Which likely stifled growth because many game-changers are administratively challenged (including me).
- Due to the high cost of color ink cartridges

> in the company's color printers, she mandated that all color copies needed to be pre-approved by her! WTF? Here we have a sales team selling multiyear, multimillion-dollar deals and they're afraid to present proposals to their prospective clients in color, for fear of angering Michelle! Are you kidding me?

As a first time CEO, Kate didn't really recognize the issue at first. She knew something was off, but she couldn't put her finger on it . . . until she heard me tell my "Who's Your Mike?" story at a Vistage leadership event. Then it clicked for her. It wasn't that Michelle was tired or needed time off—and it was no longer acceptable to simply say, "Don't worry about it, that's just Michelle. I'll go talk to her." Kate finally realized she had a full-blown Mike situation on her hands.

Drop the Mike?

Once you realize that you have a Mike, the next logical question is, "What the hell should I do?" There's obviously a paradox at the center of all this: Having Mike on your team in the early days is great. He helped get your company where it is today. But you'll eventually need next-level leaders with experience and expertise to get you where you want to go. This is a normal part of your entrepreneurial journey.

If you've promoted Mike to a key role that he simply can't handle, something HAS to change. You're going to have to have some challenging conversations and you may have to make some difficult decisions. But there's not one right answer. Every situation is different. In some cases, Mike may be willing to take a step back and admit this isn't working, or maybe he volunteers to leave for a leadership role with a smaller company. In some cases, Mike may be coachable and can either stay in his existing role and grow into it, or take a lesser role and acquiesce to a more experienced leader while he hopes to grow into a future leader (whether for your company or for a future employer).

Unfortunately, sometimes Mike simply doesn't have a role going forward. He may be super important to you personally but has become a liability professionally. In the worst-case scenario, you lose your friend and former go-to guy because you just can't reconcile the needs of the business with the complicated emotions and egos at play. No one said this would be easy.

Again, Mike doesn't necessarily have to go. In fact, in many cases, Mike can be moved into an individual contributor role and leverage his work ethic and history with the company. With Mike, like most of the characters we'll discuss here, how you handle the situation often depends on their personalities, your relationship with them, and the work that needs to get done.

In Intermission I, beginning on page 81, you'll find some tips on how to identify whether you have a Mike (or another outgrown legacy employee) on your team. For now, here are a few possible scenarios and suggestions for dealing with Mike.

Choose your own Mike adventure:

» **Mike's an A-hole.** Sorry to be the bearer of bad news, but this variety of ego-driven Mike isn't going to be comfortable taking a less prominent role. He's gotten used to being chief-of-something officer, and he's not going to give up that clout easily. Intentionally or not, he'll drive a wedge between the new leader you bring in and the rest of your team. This one may seem obvious, but it isn't always; entrepreneurs are usually an optimistic bunch, and you could miss Mike's dark side. He may show you the conciliatory, respectful friend side and only your team feels the wrath of his passive-aggressive side. We're often the last to know!

» **Mike is super talented but doesn't have strong leadership skills.** Consider asking him to move into an individual contributor role. I've seen this handled effectively many times—if Mike is humble. The best approach is candor and authenticity. Share that you believe he has an important spot on the team, but you need to identify an experienced leader who can scale the company. You're growing too fast to have him learn on the job. Consider offering him some coaching to help him develop over time—perhaps for his next gig.

» **Maybe Mike just needs a helping hand.** Rather than blow up your team, bring in a coach or mentor to help Mike grow into the role gradually. I've seen it work before. This option works best if you have other seasoned leaders on the team to fill any leadership void resulting from Mike's inexperience and time spent learning. As always, the best results start with open and honest communication. Tell him that you believe in him and want him (and the company) to be successful. Then make sure he has the tools and resources to do so.

The bottom line is that when you realize you have a Mike on your team, you're going to have to take action. Mike's in over his head, but you aren't—at least not yet. Trust me, you don't have to sink with your legacy team!

This is hard work. No one promised it wouldn't be. But if you really think about it, deep down in your heart, you're probably thinking about someone (or someones?) on your team right now. They're probably very well-intentioned and been there for you in the past. But unfortunately, they're holding you and the company back.

I like to change the perspective, partially because all this emotional stuff sucks and it's hard to make a strategic decision when you're not thinking straight. But I like to shift the conversation from a "what do we do with Mike?" to "what if we had a superstar instead of Mike?" Imagine that you have someone in that role who has been where you want to go; someone who has previously doubled or tripled a company like yours; someone who has experience negotiating multimillion-dollar deals or scaling up operations or integrating two acquisitions.

Take names out of the boxes and remove emotions for a minute. Forget about Mike, or Michelle, or Mikayla, or whoever it is. What if you could replace a low performer with someone who has the skills, expertise, and culture fit to move the company forward faster?

I don't necessarily mind learning lessons the hard way, at times. That's actually how I learn best. But it's pretty damn amazing to have someone on your team who has been through the battles, who has already learned those lessons, and has the scars to prove it. I want to leverage those lessons learned and get there faster, stronger, more efficiently. There's no reason why we need to learn all of these lessons the hard way. This entrepreneurial stuff is tough enough already!

Challenging? Yes, but a necessary part of the process if you want to professionalize your team, scale your business, and take it to the legendary next level. As my mom used to say, "If it were easy, everybody would do it."

02

HARRY THE HUSTLER

ROCKSTAR SALESPERSON . . . BAD MANAGER

"Salespeople are a different breed. Competitive. Emotional. Driven with an often myopic focus. What makes a salesperson great doesn't always translate to greatness as a manager. In fact, those attributes are often in conflict as they move into leadership."

– **Scott Leese,** 6X Sales Leader, 3X Founder and 3X Author, including *Addicted to the Process*

Many entrepreneurs fall into a common trap. As your company grows and expands, it seems only natural to promote loyal lieutenants to your newly minted leadership team. You know: the guys and gals who've been by your side every step of the way. And they know you and the business better than anyone!

But the people who've been with you from your garage to $5 million in revenue probably shouldn't be the ones on your leadership team as you strive for $10, $20, or $50 million. I advise clients that if you have a leadership team of five people—and *all of you* are going through exponential growth for the first time—you're going to learn a lot of lessons the hard way. I like to augment your leadership team with a few been-there-done-that veterans, who will help you "get there" faster, cheaper, and with less heartache.

Promoting your loyal lieutenants into leadership positions may seem like the right move—and it may be—especially if they want the promotion. But there's a different set of skills required to scale your business. Believe it or not, being a great foot soldier who performs well in the trenches doesn't necessarily make someone a great leader or strategist.

So, what do you do? These situations provide a number of challenges, and yes, some opportunities. There's definitely no boilerplate solution for dealing with people's emotions, egos, and expectations. I'll outline some of these challenges, provide a few examples, and offer some guidance and suggestions that just might help if you find yourself in a similar situation.

In this chapter, I'll focus on the sales function, but this advice can be applied to any of the departments in your organization. For example, your customer service jack-of-all-trades loyalist may not make a great VP of human resources, and your best Java developer might not have what it takes to lead a tech team. And so on.

Who Is Harry the Hustler?

Over the years I've seen so many entrepreneurial companies whose sales team consists of two people: the founder and a young, wickedly talented employee we'll call Harry the Hustler. He learns the ropes by watching you in action, soaking everything in. While he can't perfectly replicate what you do, he's got it down. And he makes it his own. He knows the product inside and out, knows the lingo, knows how to counter objections, and exudes confidence. In short, he can flat-out sell!

Over time, you come to rely on Harry to drive revenue. He's a go-getter, and there's no doubt he's responsible for much of your success. Now what? You both want the company to continue growing exponentially—but that's a lot harder to do at this next stage. Harry was great when you were starting at zero and had nowhere to go but up. But now a different skill set is needed.

This is where I've seen numerous entrepreneurs make critical mistakes with significant ramifications. You know you need to build a sales team to continue growing at this pace, which means you'll need a sales leader. So, what do you do? Many of us promote Harry, of course!

But the skills needed to be a kickass salesperson are completely different from the skills required to build, lead, and manage a next-level sales function. If you play this wrong, you might end up having to fire Harry the Crappy Manager down the road—and you will have lost Harry the Kickass Salesperson as well. Talk about a double whammy!

The Sales Leader

Because sales are usually driven by the founder's entrepreneurial spirit and the hard work of Harry the Hustler, the "plan" is often something like, "Just go hire some junior Harrys!" Then we cross our fingers and hope revenue follows. But that's not how it works. While entrepreneurial companies can get by on the backs of one or two salespeople, they need something more as they try to scale. Simply put, the heroic efforts of a few just won't get it done anymore.

To truly set yourself up for the next level, you need leadership: someone to set the sales strategy that aligns with the company's vision and plans for growth; someone to develop and execute a sales process, with commensurate tools and systems; and the icing on the cake—someone to build a great team, manage them, hold them accountable, measure results, and coach people up or out. In other words, you need to professionalize your sales function. Again, we're talking about the sales function here, but this holds true for virtually every department in your company.

Many entrepreneurs insist on simply adding bodies to the team. This may work from time to time, but over the long haul, I've seen that strategy fail more often than it works. Once you've realized you can't build a sustainable sales engine by just throwing more salespeople into a room without a strategy or systems and processes in place, you're on your way.

Good Salesperson = Good Sales Leader?

Harry probably feels like he's a lock in for the new sales leader role. He's been with you for years, and he knows he's the best salesperson. Hell, you've been telling him how important he is to the company since Day One, so he's got a bit of an ego about it too!

What makes Harry such a great salesman, anyway? Well, in addition to knowing your product and your company inside and out, he's got a crazy competitive streak, he's driven to succeed, he's tenacious, and he loves money. Don't discount this last one—especially for salespeople!

For most Harrys, being the big shot is important. When you're the go-to sales guy, making a boatload of money on commission and earning the trust of the founder—that drives you. You close a deal, celebrate, count your money, and move on to the next deal. What most successful salespeople don't realize is that there aren't many positions that provide that same level of thrill—and compensation. But when you start talking about growing the team and bringing in a sales leader, Harry immediately goes into competitive mode and wants the job.

To Promote or Not to Promote

While Harry thinks he's the obvious—if not only—choice for the job, he probably isn't. Being a leader requires a completely different skill set, temperament, and mindset than being an individual contributor. Just look at how we described the role: 1) Set the sales strategy that aligns with the company's vision and growth plans; 2) Develop and execute the sales process; 3) Implement tools and systems; and 4) Build, lead, and manage a great team. Perhaps more importantly, this position needs to be driven more by the success of the team and organization than the leader's individual success. Harry's a badass salesperson, but does he fit the sales leader description?

He probably doesn't, but founders will often overlook glaring gaps or simply feel pressured to promote Harry. Whether he's openly lobbying for the job, or you just believe you'll lose him if you don't promote him, the pressure is real! And to be fair, some traditional thinking suggests you should promote your A-players to leadership positions, right? I just don't think a star player necessarily has the tools needed to build and lead a team. How many superstar players can you think of who went on to become superstar coaches?

Let's say you promote Harry and increase his base salary substantially—both of which he finds incredibly appealing. But Harry is no longer out there hunting big game. He's hosting meetings, training new hires, and implementing a new CRM. Not only that, he's not in "eat what you kill" mode anymore. Even if his base salary doubled, he's probably making less money now that he's no longer commissioned on his own sales.

You may notice that Harry doesn't appear to be working as hard as he used to (this doesn't happen in every case, but it often does). As a salesperson, Harry busted his ass chasing that next deal. Sure, he loved the chase and wanted to please you, but he also loves money, and selling is his jam! Without the financial incentive and by doing something he's not super passionate about, Harry's work ethic is going to look different. You'll probably need to find other ways to fire him up.

To head some of this off, I've seen many entrepreneurs promote their Harry to sales leader, but structure their comp so they still earn commissions on sales they personally make. Be careful here. If Harry divvies up sales leads AND he makes commission on his deals, what prevents him from keeping the best leads for himself? There might not even be an ulterior motive—maybe he just wants to make sure the "important" ones get the VIP treatment. Does his team trust that he's doing what's best for them? There's a lot of egos on a sales team, and putting the manager in direct competition with his employees sure sounds like trouble to me.

Making the Right Choice the Wrong Way

As you read this chapter, you may be thinking, *Kurt says not to promote Harry—got it.* Well . . . not exactly. Harry's a human being, with emotions and ego. Ignoring the fact that he's interested in the job (or feels entitled to it) may be a bigger mistake than promoting him! You could look outside and potentially hire a great sales leader to build the infrastructure and the team—but NOW you pissed off your ringer! And if he won't buy into the new leader, he's as good as gone.

Just Tell Me What the Hell to Do!

Damned if you do, damned if you don't, right? Yep—welcome to leadership! Growing pains can be tricky, for sure. There are any number of ways this can play out, most of which I've witnessed firsthand. While I can't give specific advice for every possible scenario, there are some key points you should consider before making your decision.

It's important to note, no one else can make this decision for you. Every situation is unique. Sure, seek the counsel of your executive coach or YPO forum or read what Jim Collins, Gino Wickman, or Verne Harnish have to say in their best-selling books—but no one has the answer for you. You need to make the best decision with the available information.

In other chapters, I've advised you to simply cut ties with people like Pipeline Paul. Move on! He's not salvageable and it's just getting worse every day. But with Harry the Hustler, it's different. He hasn't done anything wrong. In fact, it's usually the opposite! He's been so good that you're close to promoting him into a job for which he's not qualified. Hell, if he truly knew what the role entailed, he probably wouldn't even want it!

Unfortunately, there's no silver bullet solution to this problem. But thankfully, Harry is still one of your key employees. You trust him and he trusts you. There are several approaches I've seen work here—and several that haven't worked so well.

From having an open and honest conversation about the position, to hiring Harry a coach, there are ways to keep the team engaged and build your sales organization at the same time. Let's walk through a few scenarios. Hopefully a few of them land for you.

Real-Life Examples: "Let's Make a Deal" Style

Door #1: We Made It Work

Jessica and Tom are clients I got to know through YPO. They co-founded a successful insurance business in the Midwest. Tom was the rainmaker who knew everyone in the industry, attended conferences, played golf with the movers and shakers, and sold some serious business. Jessica was the company's CEO and made sure the company delivered on Tom's promises.

You've already guessed the nuance associated with this one. Jessica's "Harry" was her partner, Tom. I mean, who better to build and run the new sales team than Tom? He wasn't only the best sales guy in the industry—he was Jessica's partner!

Tom became the sales leader and went out and hired three "junior Toms." And since his book of business was critical to the company's success, Tom was expected to continue to "carry a bag." At first, Tom loved the thrill of building his own kingdom: hiring his team, divvying up the pursuits he hadn't had time to pursue over the years, and setting his team free to conquer the world. But he quickly learned that his team struggled with ambiguity—they couldn't make shit up like Tom did.

Turns out that his new hires required some actual training and, you know, things like sales collateral, case studies, and a sales process. He spent an inordinate amount of time holding their hands. They weren't successful by any measure, and his personal numbers tanked.

He doubled down as a sales manager. He implemented a CRM to provide data and tried holding his team accountable to metrics, key performance indicators, and the like. He sat in on more internal meetings, sales calls, and customer meetings. He wanted to figure out what the hell was wrong!

He was in his own living hell. There's nothing worse for a kickass salesperson than to find himself conducting internal meetings and tracking their team's calls. AARRGGHH! Not only was Tom doing things he hated, he wasn't doing the things he loved. He was a relationship guy who loved the art of the deal. The last thing he wanted to do was sit in his office and review call reports!

Long story short, Jessica not only saw the numbers decreasing every month, but she knew Tom well enough to know he was struggling and not having fun. Thankfully, their relationship was strong and could handle the open and honest discussion they needed to have.

Tom went back to being a rainmaker and, once he got over the perceived demotion and realized how much more he enjoyed life in this role, he got on board with bringing in a sales leader from the outside. He could be a resource for the sales leader, mentor new hires—AND make it rain!

Obviously, Laura's Harry is different from most, but many of the above points are valid for your situation. I could argue that her case was more challenging than yours because she essentially had to demote a partner and co-founder. Talk about stressful!

The key to Jessica and Tom's success was the relationship they had. She knew Tom wasn't happy, and he trusted that Jessica had his back. With a solid relationship foundation, retaining Harry to do what he does best and bringing in a next-level leader is absolutely possible.

Door #2: What Not to Do

Laura runs a successful company that caters to the corporate office and commercial real estate market. In the early days, she drove sales through her network. Her Harry was one of her first employees, who demonstrated a knack for sales from the get-go. He tagged along with Laura and soon took over many of her relationships and built his own—freeing up Laura to run the company.

The market was HOT, and Harry was on fire! But Laura had her own Harry the Hustler decision to make as the company grew. She made the decision she felt was in the company's best interest. She looked outside for a sales leader, a builder of teams. She decided Harry wasn't cut out for leadership. He was young and temperamental, and she needed him right where he was—delivering new customers.

Unfortunately, Laura didn't communicate with Harry, so he was blindsided. True, she was the CEO and wasn't required to consult with her employee about bringing in his boss, but remember, we're dealing with human beings here: human beings with emotions and egos, hopes and dreams.

She ended up recruiting an amazing leader who built all the things we've been discussing, including a kickass team. Sadly, the new sales leader had to build the company's next-level team without Harry. He resigned out of frustration six months later and took many of his customer relationships with him. I think she could have kept Harry and they could have successfully worked together for many years if she had been more open and honest with him during this process.

Door #3: You Can Do It

Suzi founded and ran a high-flying technology company. She was a big fan of her "Harriett the Hustler" and wanted to give her every chance to grow in her career. When Suzi decided she needed a sales leader she discussed it with Harriett, and they mutually decided on a creative solution.

They both agreed Harriett wasn't currently ready for the role but felt like she had the capacity to do it with the proper training and coaching. They decided to bring in a sales strategist on a consulting basis to help build the strategic aspects of the sales function. In the meantime, they sought out a sales-minded executive coach who could serve as Harriett's mentor for the next twelve to twenty-four months.

I could argue that Suzi's company could have reached its goals faster and with fewer hiccups if she had brought in an experienced sales leader from the outside. But she also eliminated much of the risk of introducing an outsider into the company and culture. While there are many reasons to seek the been-there-done-that veteran, there are pros to promoting from within and putting your faith behind your team. But it's not for the faint at heart. There's a lot that should go into making the final decision. Things like Harriet's growth potential and strategic capabilities, shifting her sales quota to members of the team, and her ability to transition from individual contributor to future leader, are just a few of the things to consider.

One Size Does NOT Fit All

Obviously, there is no right or wrong answer for your own Harry situation—and there are pros and cons with any decision you make. This definitely falls into the more-art-than-science department! A few things to keep in mind:

1. **Know your goals and what it will take to achieve them.** Knowing this helps you understand what you need out of your new position.
2. **Understand Harry's goals.** Does he want a title, more money, equity, prestige, flexibility? Knowing this will help you understand his motivations—what he truly wants.
3. **Invest in him.** Consider hiring an executive coach or maybe pay for his MBA. Find ways to help him achieve his long-term goals.
4. **Remember, he's a human being and a big part of your success.** Be open, honest, and empathetic. He's going through a range of emotions and needs to know you have his back.

For more tips, tidbits, and insights into Harry the Hustler and other legacy employees, check out Intermission I, beginning on page 81.

CEO
RITA

03

RIGHT-HAND RITA

YOUR LEGACY LIEUTENANT

"Avoid talent headaches by embracing and communicating early that managing business growth is an inadequate development tool for the next big leadership role. These roles are critical change agents to speed, efficiency, and innovation. Leadership positions shouldn't be used as development roles for loyalists. Can they get there? Yes—through proactive investments in education, coaches, and networks. Until then, hire leaders that make them, and YOU, better. Own that the CEO is the caretaker of enterprise health so that everyone wins, not individuals."

– **Craig Wiley,** Founder and CEO, Transcend

Rita started out as your administrative assistant. She would do everything from managing your schedule and doing your filing to picking up your dry cleaning and your much-needed lattés. Over the years, her responsibilities grew to include things like ordering office supplies, manning the front desk, and managing your email. This led to the official title of office manager, as well as de facto protector of your schedule. No one gets through Rita without her approval. She feels like she's an extension of you, and whatever she says goes.

As your company grew, Rita grew with you and took on anything and everything you needed. Now as you continue to grow and scale, she wants the big title—VP of Operations. She thinks she's earned it, and you feel loyal to her because of all the hard work she's put in through the years. But you probably need a next-level VP of Operations: someone who's done that job before, not someone who'll be learning on the job. You don't want your team to learn too many lessons the hard way. It will inevitably stunt your growth.

But Rita doesn't see things this way and pushes for more. However, like other characters in this book, just because someone helped you get where you are today doesn't necessarily mean they're the right leader to take you where you want to go.

So, what do you do with Rita? She's been incredibly loyal and has been in the foxhole with you for so many years. Do you reward her with a title and responsibilities and let her fall on her face? Or do you recruit a "next-level" VP of Operations to help you get there faster and with fewer hiccups?

For the purpose of this chapter, Rita was an administrative assistant who grew into an operations leader role, but many other examples of legacy employees who have contributed mightily and "climbed the ladder" exist. If any of this resonates with you—and I have no doubt it will—read on for some stories, tips, and tidbits.

The Importance of Team Members Who Just Figure Things Out

My entrepreneurial friends and clients are a wildly diverse group of people. Some are visionary leaders who are dreaming up the products we'll be using five to ten years down the road, while others love nothing more than pitching their business to prospective customers. Then there are those who love building great processes, systems, and teams. They come in all shapes, sizes, colors, and creeds, but the successful ones often have one thing in common—they have kickass "right-hands" who do whatever it takes to get things done!

I'm not necessarily talking about an assistant to manage your schedule and answer the phone, though those are important too. I'm talking about someone who's a critical part of the team throughout the startup phase: someone who handles all the tactical or administrative "stuff" so you can focus on building your business.

You can't do everything on your own. As someone who's tried it before, let me assure you—you can't, nor should you. Many entrepreneurs feel like they can't afford an assistant or think it's a luxury. But trust me, having a great assistant can make all the difference in your life as CEO.

When you find someone with the right mix of hunger and ambition who is hard-working and willing to learn on the job, you're golden. A good assistant handles many tasks, from scheduling meetings and drafting memos, to picking up lunch, setting up the Wi-Fi, or changing the printer ink. You may be thinking, *I can take out my own trash! Why would I spend money on that?* But it's not about taking out the trash. It's about freeing you up to focus on bigger things to drive your business.

With the right assistant, you can trust all the "stuff" will be handled without your oversight. You can focus on developing the product or new markets, creating the strategy, or leading the team. This is not necessarily an easy hire. You need someone to take this journey with you: ideally, someone with traits like curiosity, grit, and work ethic; someone who is a problem-solver and self-motivated. The adage "hire slow, fire fast" definitely applies here.

Enter Right-Hand Rita

You might be ahead of the curve and already have a badass person in that role. If you have one, Rita is almost literally your right-hand. She's a workhorse. She's loyal. She's hungry. And she seems to relish taking on new challenges and developing new skills.

Rita may have come to you as an intern or maybe her mom is a member of a leadership organization you belong to. She probably started out doing many of the mundane tasks I described above. But she's come a long way as the company's grown.

You quickly came to rely on Rita for everything. She not only took on every task, but she also anticipated your needs and did things without being asked. And she did everything RIGHT! You didn't even have to check her work, you knew she was on top of it. You trust her with your money and your life.

Over time, your team grew from four to twenty employees and Rita was there, willing and eager to help, adding responsibilities along the way. Now, she's not just managing the office, she's choosing a new office for the company, negotiating with landlords and furniture suppliers, and managing the move.

Rita's a self-starter, and she simply gets shit done. As you've grown, she's grown with you. She wants to be in the trenches right next to you, and you're intensely loyal to each other. You've grown beyond your imagination, and you know you wouldn't be where you are without her.

And this is exactly when the situation can turn problematic.

The Inflection Point

When you grow beyond the startup phase, you need to gear up for a different stage of growth. In the early days, your team included a bunch of generalists who were doing a bit of everything to make it happen. You relied on your own grit and determination, along with do-it-all employees like Mike, Harry the Hustler, and, of course, Right-Hand Rita. She's been by your side, taking things off your plate, and learning to do things she had never done before—with gusto. But you've hit a point where you need to professionalize your organization: create structure, move from generalists to specialists, and recruit experienced leaders to drive growth.

This is a good time to remind you about the importance of adding experience to your team at this stage. I'm a big believer in bringing in a few leaders from the outside who've already been through what you're about to, as your business scales. Leverage the mistakes from THEIR past to help you get there faster and minimize mistakes. It doesn't mean you need to replace your entire team. But, as we talked about with Harry the Hustler—if your leadership team is all going through this exponential growth for the first time, you'll learn a lot of lessons the hard way.

Is Rita Ready to Be a VP?

Rita has admittedly nailed everything she's taken on thus far. And she's not-so-subtly telling you that she wants to be promoted to the VP of Operations position you recently created. She knows the business better than anyone, and she's practically been running operations for the last three years anyway. Without her, you'd be lost.

But when you're trying to grow at a rapid pace and professionalize your business, Rita's probably not the right person for that role—at least right now. Why do I think it's not her right now? Because the stakes are too high. You don't have time for her to learn lessons the hard way; you need to go faster. If this is your first time growing a business at this size and pace, you're in uncharted territory. You can't have everyone around you learning the ropes with you! You need some experience on the team to help you lead. You don't have time for a key leader to be learning on the job.

It's possible that Rita could grow into a killer operations leader, but not without help. She doesn't know what she doesn't know, and you don't have the time nor the experience to help her develop those skills. Dangit, you're just trying to figure all this stuff out yourself!

What to Do about Rita

In my years working with entrepreneurs at Ernst & Young, The Controller Group, and HireBetter, I've seen this situation play out in a number of ways—some good, and some . . . well . . . not so good. I can't tell you how many times I've had a CEO call us to upgrade their Right-Hand Rita outright. I've also seen CEOs promote Rita and wonder why she's falling well short of expectations. After all, "Rita always came through before," they say.

While there are definitely some wrong ways to handle this, there's not necessarily a single right way, either. Remember, you're dealing with emotions and egos here—hell, even their hopes and dreams. Things can go off track for a million reasons that are hard to prepare for or predict. But there are ways you can approach Rita to help ensure her loyalty, hard work, and expertise are acknowledged and appreciated, and she remains with the company, even if you ultimately decide promoting her isn't the right move.

My first word of advice here is to communicate with appreciation and honesty—leveraging the trust and respect you've developed over the years. If you have a foundation of trust and respect and an open line of communication with Rita, the conversations I'm about to describe will come easier. If nothing else, Rita has earned your honest assessment of the situation. Don't simply say to yourself, "She's never done it before so she can't run the entire operation" and bring someone in above her. Again, we're dealing with egos and emotions, and without communicating effectively, you're not being fair to Rita, and you may very well lose her.

For more tips and things to consider, refer to Intermission I, beginning on page 81.

I Love and Appreciate You, AND We Need Some Next-Level Leadership to Help Us Both

Speaking for myself here, I'm not an operationally minded guy. I'm not driven by the day-to-day, by the important details that keep the trains running on time. And many of my entrepreneurial friends aren't either. I'm driven by the big picture, the ideas that come in the middle of the night, the relationships and thrill of the chase. It's why Gino Wickman suggests pairing up people like me (whom he terms "Visionaries") with operational gurus (or "Integrators"). It's also why I've never been the right person to lead and mentor an up-and-coming operational leader.

In one of my previous businesses, I personally faced a similar situation. I had a killer right-hand person who had risen through the ranks to be so much more, and he wanted to be my next COO. I had a conversation with him that eventually led to my realization that it wasn't necessarily that he couldn't do the job, but he needed guidance and mentorship that only another operationally-minded leader could provide. I told him we needed someone who could both lead the company with proven capabilities AND develop him to be the operational leader that we BOTH wanted him to become.

In my case, I relied on the trust we built over several years. But while every situation is different, I've seen enough Right-Hand Ritas with clients and colleagues to know that my case wasn't unique. If Rita isn't the right fit at this time, but you believe in her and want to see her grow into the VP role, then that's a conversation you should have. Just know that it takes a big person to accept they aren't ready—self-awareness and a dedication to personal growth aren't as prevalent as one would hope in the world. But if Rita sees that you're offering the opportunity to grow and develop skills under the tutelage of a leader who can nurture her growth, then it CAN be a match made in heaven.

Please be honest with Rita. Do you see a path toward a leadership role at your company? Maybe Rita is ready for that jump in two or three years working with an experienced mentor as a boss? Don't promise anything you can't deliver, but lay out your vision for her, so she can see that you're investing in her future as well as making the best decision for the business. Perhaps explain to Rita that learning under an operational leader, who is a true coach and mentor, will make her extremely marketable as an operational leader down the road. If you create a culture of personal and professional development, Rita will know that you're looking out for her.

Sometimes, no matter how good your intentions are, Rita won't be able to handle the information. She might threaten to leave if she doesn't get what she "deserves." And she may actually leave—or do a lot of huffing and puffing! But that may mean she wasn't ready to lead the team anyway and wasn't mature enough to develop those skills under an experienced leader. This doesn't necessarily mean any negative reaction automatically makes Rita unfit to lead a team. Remember, we're dealing with people and their emotions as well as the image of the future they envisioned.

Does Promoting Rita *Ever* Work?

In the past, I've had clients and friends insist they HAVE to promote their Rita to a leadership position. And admittedly, it has "worked out" a few times. But it's hard to fully define what success is in these cases, so let's look at a couple of them, side by side.

Jeff was a HireBetter client who was expanding his team to grow from $5 million in revenue to $20 million over the next three years. He had started out in his garage and bootstrapped his way into a real success story, so convincing him to spend the kind of money needed to hire experienced leaders was a challenge. He felt he had the makings of a leadership team among his rag-tag group of college buddies and loyal lieutenants who got him there. Among that group was one he was especially high on—his former assistant, current office manager, and wannabe VP of Operations—his "Rita."

After a number of Strategic Talent Planning™ sessions and a lot of soul-searching, we mutually determined it was time to bring in an experienced operational leader to drive growth. But Jeff ultimately couldn't make the hard decision. Rita wanted the job, campaigned for it, and virtually threatened to quit if she didn't get it. Jeff decided to double down on Rita. She threw herself into learning how to be the best VP of Operations she could possibly be at that stage in her career.

But after a year in her new role, it became clear that

Rita was struggling. Jeff wasn't able to offer guidance or direction on how to be a leader—he was learning how to be one himself. He did, however, finally take our advice and invest in a hands-on executive coach for her: a coach with an operational mindset who had the relevant experience to help her with everything from leadership development to team-building to accountability, while providing the tools and resources to help her do her job. They met regularly, and the coach became a de facto member of the team.

Over the next twenty-four months, Rita grew both professionally and personally, and the company doubled to over $10 million in revenue. Although not reaching the $20 million Jeff wanted to achieve, he would absolutely tell you that his Rita "worked out" and would sing her praises. But would he have achieved his $20 million goal if he had brought in an operational leader for Rita to report to and learn from? Would they have made fewer mistakes along the way? We'll never know.

In another case, Jack had the hard conversation with his "Roger" and commenced the search for a chief operating officer who had experience growing a company similar to Jack's: someone who also had the capacity and personality to become a true mentor to Roger—and the rest of the team. Jack's goal was to grow his company from $6.5 to $15 million and get acquired as soon as possible, as his industry was evolving at breakneck speed.

Roger was understanding and receptive. He went from running operations to reporting to the new COO and becoming more of an individual contributor. But one of Jack's requirements for the new COO was to coach and develop Roger's skills so that he could become a COO or VP of Operations when the opportunity was right. Three years later, the company was acquired, and Jack gladly helped Roger find his new home as the COO of a peer's company in town. Both parties got exactly what they wanted: Roger got to hone his skills into a badass COO, and Jack benefited from his work in an operational support role and as culture champion. And along the way, the company ultimately achieved Jack's revenue goals and a very nice exit, which benefitted Jack and Roger financially too.

Just goes to show you there's not one right answer, and there are trade-offs with almost any decision you make with regard to your Right-Hand Rita. For more insights into Rita and other legacy employees, please refer to Intermission I, beginning on page 81.

04

SIDE-HUSTLE SAM

THE ASPIRING ENTREPRENEUR

"My business started out as a side hustle. Now I'm an entrepreneur with my own team—so I understand both sides of the coin with the new gig economy! I've found that if you communicate with your team and help them achieve their goals, they'll help you achieve yours!"

– **Kit Rich,** Entrepreneur, founder of KICHGO and fitness trainer to the stars

Ah, the early days of a startup . . . You're trying to get your company off the ground, and everyone's figuring things out. You need team members who're just as entrepreneurial as you are: employees who are driven and gritty, always on, and will do whatever needs to be done. If you think about it, most of your employees are probably risk-takers. They're placing a bet on your startup, just like you are. They think it has a chance to make it and give them a chance to cash in.

This entrepreneurial spirit is what makes them great employees at this stage. But it also makes them more likely to be interested in developing a side business. After all, they're essentially entrepreneurs too. Side hustles can be tricky for the entrepreneur and the leadership team to navigate. I actually think they can work—but not always.

I've seen side hustles go wrong when there's an air of secrecy or if the side hustle gets in the way of the main hustle. But they can also go well if there's a foundation of trust, respect, and communication between the employee and the leadership team. In this chapter, I'll explore a few good examples and a few bad ones—and I'll offer some advice for navigating these waters.

Meet Side-Hustle Sam

Sam has read numerous books about real estate investing, and now he's building a burgeoning empire on the side by buying, renovating, and leasing single-family homes. Or maybe he's running an art boutique on Main Street with his wife. Or he's working on an app with his business-school classmate—an app to aggregate the best hunting and fishing sites in North America. It really doesn't matter. All you know is that he seems to be in the office less and less, especially now that you have embraced a virtual work environment. He definitely seems to be embracing more of the "virtual" than the "work" part!

Before we throw Sam in the trash, maybe there's an opportunity to actually help him realize his dream. Maybe even help him get started financially, as long as he helps you realize your dreams. Your approach is basically, "Give me all you've got while you're here and help me achieve X, and I'll support you, mentor you, help you achieve Y. But take advantage of me, lie to me, or steal from me, and I can't get rid of you fast enough." Side-Hustle Sam may be in your midst already, or he may be on your horizon. Let's explore this unspoken part of the entrepreneurial world.

My Story

Before I became an entrepreneur and founded and exited several successful ventures, I began my career as an accountant at Ernst & Young. I was very fortunate! To be honest, I wasn't exactly the most decorated student at the University of Arkansas business school (I like to tell people, "I was only a couple of points shy of a 4.0 grade point average!") and I didn't have an MBA. But I leveraged my network for an opportunity and also passed the CPA exam, which gave EY the confidence that I could do the job. They took a chance on me.

Working as an auditor for a "Big Four" public accounting firm taught me some valuable lessons. First and foremost, that I'm a crappy accountant! My job at EY also gave me access to clients' C-suites, which opened my eyes to the types of challenges facing middle-market leaders. While I didn't love number-crunching and pure audit work, I did love asking questions, listening, and connecting leaders with people smarter than me to solve their problems. But what became most apparent to me during my four years at EY was I needed MORE. There was an entrepreneur inside of me who wanted out!

I often look back on my time with EY, wondering what might have been if I had ignored my inner entrepreneur and remained an accountant. One thing I know for sure—I eventually would have been uncovered as a shitty accountant! Or maybe I would have just started a side hustle like so many other would-be entrepreneurs: that passion project which, if successful, eventually leads to a fork in the road: give up on your entrepreneurial dream or dive in headfirst and burn your boat.

As for me, I left public accounting for a job promising dotcom riches in 1999. But it was the dotcom crash in 2000 that left me out of a job and practically forced me to follow my entrepreneurial dream. I'm one of the lucky ones. Sure, there were a lot of bumps, bruises, and mistakes along the way, but the entrepreneur in me ultimately won out.

Many entrepreneurs have a similar story. They take whatever job they can out of school to get their foot in the door and put food on the table—then they end up determining that the corporate world isn't for them. Others got their entrepreneurial start when they lost their job, leaving them no choice but to make it happen. Others got started when their passion project showed promise.

Side Hustles Happen

As I said, leaders of early-stage companies need to surround themselves with entrepreneurs! They need other people with a can-do spirit, who they can trust to get things done: people like Bounce-Around Betty, Harry the Hustler, and Right-Hand Rita.

If entrepreneurs are naturally attracted to side gigs—and startups need entrepreneurial employees—a paradox arises. You need people LIKE YOU, who are driven, passionate, and want to make big things happen. But how can you expect your team of entrepreneurs not to have outside interests and big dreams of their own? The short answer is that you'll likely attract employees who develop outside interests, especially since virtual work environments make it easier to manage side hustles.

Many of you probably know a Side-Hustle Sam personally. Some can balance their two worlds, some can't. Some are shady and will lie to your face to hide what they're doing, while others will be open and honest with you. How you decide to handle these situations is entirely up to you. Predictably, there's usually a bit more art than science involved.

> Before we dig in—a public service announcement. I don't want to tell you how to run your company, but if you want to get it off the ground, you can't have a team of rule-followers who ask permission before doing anything. You need some mavericks who make things happen! And if you want a gun-slinging spirit inside the company, be prepared to expect it outside of it as well.

No Two Sams Are Alike

Your own Side-Hustle Sam experience will look different,

depending on a number of variables. Your industry, company culture, your personality, and your particular Sam's personality will all factor into the relationship you build. In certain industries, side hustles are almost built into the actual job.

For example, real estate is ripe for side hustles, as are the gaming and technology industries. Real estate is obvious, because that industry attracts dealmakers. As for the other two—in both cases, you've got a creative and tech-minded team designing and building your end-product. Along the way, one of your employees conceives of an idea that doesn't end up making your development list or is for something unrelated to the company. It can be fairly common for employees to want to keep working on that idea or their passion project in their spare time.

Side projects spring up in other industries too. One CEO friend of mine had an employee develop a new internal timecard system for the company. After the employee built a beta version for in-house use, both she and the CEO realized that this met a huge need in the industry and, with a little bit more polishing, could be developed into its own business! They ended up partnering on that venture and eventually sold their "side gig" for over $200 million.

Now, not every side gig turns into $200 million, but you get the point. A different CEO might have told her, "No, you finished the project, now get back to your day job." Or a different employee might have finished the project and left the company to focus on developing her timecard technology. The employee might have had a $200 million idea but lacked the business acumen and capital needed to turn it into reality. In the example above, though, the employer/employee relationship and their mutual candor led to a very successful outcome.

Side-Hustle Sam in Action: The Good, the Bad, and the Ugly

The Good

Ryan is a client who owns a real estate development company that specializes in townhomes and apartments with a great environment for college students: the kinds of places your kids want to live in when they go off to college.

In the early-early days, his team consisted of him (the intrepid founder) and Samantha, the hard-working, relentless dealmaker. As Ryan managed the company and dealt with marketing, courting investors, and keeping the lights on, Samantha was on the road scouting, haggling, and purchasing new properties to convert into upscale housing near college campuses. She was AMAZING at her job: a natural born wheeler-and-dealer. The company grew rapidly behind their efforts.

But while Samantha was out of the office working for Ryan, she came across other real-estate opportunities: a commercial lot begging for a gas station; an old fast-food restaurant that could be fixed up and flipped; or strip malls across town. Samantha wasn't sure how to handle these opportunities. She was on the clock when she found them and wanted to keep everything above-board. She also knew Ryan had experience and money, and in the back of her mind, she felt like they could do more together than she could by digging into her own shallow pockets.

Samantha wanted Ryan to know she was being presented with opportunities. She said something along the lines of, "While I was researching the Maple Street condos, the seller asked if I was interested in his commercial lot across town. I told him we don't do non-residential, but he insisted I take a look. He's having liquidity challenges—it looks like a good deal."

Ryan appreciated her honesty and gave her his blessing to pursue deals from time to time—just let him know when she did. Ryan's approach was, "As long as she rocks it for me, I don't care what else she does!" They kept communicating and determined that the market was right to do more of these side deals, so they became partners. Ryan provided the seed money, expertise, and contacts, and Samantha provided sweat equity and non-stop hustle to do great work for both her day job and her side projects. Fast-forward to today, and Samantha is the lead dealmaker for Ryan's burgeoning student housing company AND they're partners in a commercial real estate holding company!

> The key to Samantha and Ryan's success was the trust they built early on. She was comfortable sharing with him her interest in pursuing side deals, and he trusted Samantha—that she would continue to shine for the company. While they didn't expect these side deals to negatively impact the business, they knew they'd fig-

> ure out a solution if they did. It helped that Ryan was a financial partner in the side deals! Obviously, this can be a recipe for disaster if the main business tanks or their relationship goes south; but you're an entrepreneur, you're optimistic, and if things don't go well, that's a problem for future Ryan!

The Bad

Instead of looking at 2020 as the "Year of the Pandemic," you could look at it as the "Year of the Side Hustle," as side gigs popped up everywhere. Most companies sent employees home, and many initially had no plan to hold employees accountable. In other words, some of your employees took advantage of the situation and started a side hustle, on your dime!

In one of my CEO Forums—groups I set up to help leaders navigate the pandemic by sharing struggles, advice, and opportunities—Enrique shared he was having trouble with an employee, Samuel. Several months into the shutdown, Enrique noticed that Samuel's work wasn't up to snuff. His final reports weren't polished and seemed cobbled together at the last minute, almost an afterthought.

But damn, did Samuel know how to put up a front! He was always the first one on team Zoom calls and made a grand showing when it was his turn to share what he was working on. He talked a big game, but something was off. Enrique's antenna was up.

Meanwhile, Samuel's actual work product deteriorated, and other team members started making comments. His niceties and Zoom flair stopped covering up for work deficiencies. His next tactic appeared to be showering Enrique with praise. Phrases like, "You're such an amazing leader" and "We're so lucky you're guiding the ship during the pandemic." When I hear this type of flowery praise, I start thinking that they're full of shit. It's usually a tactic to deflect their poor performance!

After missing several key deadlines, Enrique decided enough was enough and confronted Samuel about his performance. Samuel quit on the spot! He didn't want to be held accountable, and we later found out about his side project (leveraging his wife's hospital contacts to broker million-dollar deals for PPE during the peak of the pandemic), which was doing quite well.

The Ugly

This one's personal! Several years ago, "Sammy" worked for me in business development. The nature of his work had him out of the office—a lot. And honestly, I wanted him out of the office, meeting with clients and prospects. I just needed him to sell.

When he wasn't in the office or with a client, I did expect him to be available by phone. But over time, he became harder to reach. He stopped calling in and stopped putting his notes in the system. When I was able to catch up with him, he always seemed busy, like he was late for something.

Over time, Sammy's approach became untenable. I noticed him abusing the "I have a meeting at 10:00 a.m., so I'm not coming in before that" excuse. Except that his first meeting wasn't until 2:00 p.m.! I had no clue what he was doing instead, but I hated feeling like I had to inspect his calendar to find out!

I reached a point where I couldn't count on him and, more importantly, I didn't trust him. We were counting on full effort, and we weren't getting it. To be honest, this went on much longer than it should have. (Have I mentioned that I suck at holding people accountable?)

I found myself micromanaging him, which I hate doing. I examined his calendar and call reports, even checked with clients I knew to "see how my team is doing." In one case, I saw he had a breakfast meeting with a prospect on his calendar. I knew this couldn't be right, because I was meeting the prospect for a morning run at that same time!

I confronted Sammy. He was initially defiant and tried to maintain the lie until he realized he was simply digging himself a deeper hole. He admitted falsifying appointments so he could work on his rental properties. You see, his side gig was buying dumpy properties, rehabbing them, and renting them out—all while he was on my payroll. Solid investment for him, but not cool at all!

Needless to say, that was the end of the road for Sammy. No salvaging our relationship. I can deal with a lot, but not if you break my trust. It didn't have to be this way. If he had told me about the rental properties or his struggles, instead of firing him, I probably would have suggested that he hire a property manager—and I may have even invested in his properties!

The Big Picture

As an entrepreneur myself, I've learned you can't—nor should you want to—kill your employees' entrepreneurial spirit. That spirit helps make them solid early-stage employees. In my years working with entrepreneurial companies, I've realized that having a reputation as an incubator for future entrepreneurs is a great talent magnet for your company. Talented people want to work for leaders who'll develop them and help them reach their goals, as well. The way I see it, your team is helping you achieve your dreams; shouldn't you help them take steps toward achieving theirs?

While there's no single solution to handling side hustles, leaders should keep a few things in mind when dealing with them, including their relationship with employees. That relationship, built on trust, respect, and communication, will allow you to trust them to do their job regardless of their side interests. Trust is a two-way street, and you want your employees to trust you too.

The second key is the culture of accountability I preach in other chapters. Thankfully, we're not in 2020 anymore and things are shifting back to "normal," whatever that means. But HireBetter, like many others, has gone completely and "permanently" virtual. Driving accountability in a virtual world is hard. But if you have the culture and the systems in place to drive accountability, you won't spend as much time worrying, "Can I trust that

Sam is actually working from home?"

> I was recently participating in a CEO forum when I heard this nugget from a participant bragging about how he kept his young sales leader happy. He got him an Amex Black Card with a credit limit equal to the employee's monthly salary—essentially helping him with his own side hustle.
>
> Paraphrasing, he said, "Sam enjoys the night life, and he likes to feel important, so I got him a Black Card. He throws it down on the bar and acts like the big cheese. In addition to feeling important, I think it helps him with the ladies. I don't think he'll ever leave me."
>
> Not sure this is the type of incentive I'd want to offer, but it's one entrepreneur's creative way to keep his Side-Hustle Sam happy and engaged.

Just make sure you know yourself. If you're like me and holding people accountable isn't your strong suit, employees may take advantage of you to work their side hustle, or maybe their "no hustle." And if that's you, consider partnering with someone who's good at creating that culture of accountability. We'll discuss this concept more in depth in chapters 11 and 12.

Some of you are probably thinking, *You've lost your damn mind! There's no room for side hustles in MY company.* And that's OK. Just make sure you maintain open and honest communication about that with your employees and candidates. You may miss out on some talented folks, but I've seen some very successful companies with that mantra. There's definitely not only one right answer.

For additional ideas on dealing with employees like Side-Hustle Sam, check out Intermissions I and II, beginning on pages 81 and 135, respectively.

05

BOUNCE-AROUND BETTY

YOUR JACK-(OR JILL)-OF-ALL-TRADES

"When we started out, our team could do a little bit of everything. For many of them we were their first professional job. As the company grew, we did outgrow some employees and recruited specialists in key roles. But we're also very proud of the number of early employees who grew exponentially and are now key leaders in the organization."

– **John Flynn,** Open Lending CEO and EY Entrepreneur of the Year 2019

Startups usually don't have a lot—of money, resources, time—really much of anything. Most of the time, the founder has a great idea and a couple of friends or associates to help figure out how to move that idea toward reality. The "team" consists of whomever the founder has nearby: a ragtag bunch that could be trusted to at least try and figure things out. Since there's usually not much money, whatever problems arise, whatever needs to get done, you and your team have to figure it out on a shoestring. You have no choice.

When your startup gains traction and looks like it might make it, it's usually the direct result of the heroic efforts of these early team members. With few exceptions, there's usually a tireless jack-(or jill)-of-all-trades who knows a little about everything. But more importantly, they've got a figure-it-out mentality and they're willing to learn and scrap and claw to get it done. In fact, I don't think I've EVER seen a startup that's "made it" without a few of these folks on the team.

Meet Bounce-Around Betty. She's been there since day one, she's an amazing person, and she's willing to do whatever it takes to get things done. You need someone to tackle creating your startup's logo and your first set of business cards? She's on it. There's a problem with the supply chain? Betty will be on the first flight out tomorrow morning. Need to figure out the witchcraft that is Google Analytics or advertising on Facebook? She'll dive in and learn the digital marketing basics to get you started. Whenever you need something challenging done, Betty jumps right in, headfirst, without knowing whether she'll sink or swim.

These types of people are AMAZING assets in the early days. As I mentioned, you need these guys and gals in order to survive scrappy startup hell. Finding and utilizing people like Betty are key to making your business successful. If this book was about helping would-be entrepreneurs start a business, I'd spend a whole chapter encouraging you to go FIND this person and convince them to come work for you. ASAP!

But this book is for entrepreneurs who are trying to grow and scale their companies. And as you grow and begin to "professionalize" your business, your needs in each functional area will outgrow the experience and knowledge of your legacy generalists. As you begin rebranding and overhauling your website, you realize that Betty's marketing knowledge probably topped out with laying out the business cards. As you seek to own the direct-to-consumer e-commerce channel, a couple of sporadic Facebook ads won't cut it anymore. You'll likely reach the point where it becomes apparent that your secret weapon is truly a master of none!

In most cases, Betty can still be a great employee for your growing company, assuming she doesn't lose that drive, that eagerness to learn, and that willingness to do whatever it takes that made her your go-to employee early on. But problems occur when we either promote Betty beyond her capacity or her role is so ambiguous it causes confusion and problems with the rest of the team. In this chapter, I'll offer advice for how to keep Betty's (and your company's) best interests in mind as you grow beyond the everyone-does-whatever-it-takes era. I'll also share stories from clients and friends who handled this situation well—and some who didn't. I'm quite confident Betty will resonate with you.

The Swiss Army Knife

A good friend of mine, Tom, owns an e-commerce company that's taken the online world by storm. He offers a quality product at a lower-than-retail price by utilizing a direct-to-consumer business model. His company now does close to $80 million in annual revenue, employs more than a hundred people, and sells its products all over the world. It's safe to say that he's made it.

But early on, it was just Tom and his first employee—let's call her Betty—sitting in a WeWork office space, trying to figure things out on the fly. Tom knew Betty from the neighborhood, but he didn't know much about her education or job experience. She sure didn't know much about running a business, but hell, neither did Tom! They worked well together, and Tom knew he could trust Betty to learn and work her ass off—right alongside him.

The first major hurdle for the company was solving some sourcing challenges they were having with their product. Betty took point, driving down to Mexico to tour their production facility, research alternatives, and sort out the logistics of what would become their supply chain. She made things happen. By the end of her trip, she had a production deal lined up with a local factory and had sourced raw materials to boot!

When she returned to Austin, she jumped right into her next task. The founder's plan was to disrupt the existing industry by selling directly to consumers, utilizing a robust e-commerce engine. The problem was, he didn't know how to build that engine. And he certainly couldn't afford to hire someone who did! They couldn't even afford a consultant. So, he called in his one-woman cavalry, and Betty was on the case.

In a matter of weeks, Betty went from using her high school Spanish classes to strike deals in Mexico to researching SEO, learning Facebook and Google algorithms, and playing around with HubSpot. She eventually figured out the basics of digital marketing and advertising and was the lynchpin for the initial success that Tom's company had in selling their product.

As the company grew, Tom knew he needed to continue feeding the beast. He reached a point where he could afford an experienced e-commerce marketing specialist, and felt he needed to make that move. Betty was great at getting the ball rolling and proving the concept, but Tom knew he needed a focused strategic marketing plan, and team. Betty understood this and was perfectly happy to move on to the next thing that needed fixing—customer experience.

Together, Betty and Tom researched other companies' fulfillment and customer service engines, and designed their own based on what they liked and didn't like. Betty jumped right in like she always did, and quickly had a solid prototype in place!

As the company grew, Tom found himself replacing Betty at every turn. She was great at getting things going, but she wasn't the right person to lead these functional areas as they grew beyond the startup phase. Like Tom, Betty was learning as she went. The company needed next-level leaders to push the pace of growth and make his vision a reality.

In Tom's case, Betty was happy to accept the next challenge when it arose. She didn't seem to mind being replaced as head of marketing or manufacturing or customer service when it was determined that an experienced leader was necessary in each of those functions to support their pace of growth.

In the end, they realized their growth meant her "bounce-around" days might be numbered. Tom, who was also experiencing this type of growth for the first time, wanted to help her progress. He asked her what she wanted to do for her career and the company, because he felt she had earned the right to choose her own path (within reason). Betty was most interested in operations, and she had a gift for it. They ultimately moved her into that department, but not as the leader. She ended up working for a new chief operating officer Tom brought in as an experienced leader. One of the key criteria Tom had when selecting his new COO was someone who could be a great mentor and coach to his team and help them advance their careers—including, and especially, Betty.

Outgrowing Your Betty

Having a Betty on your team is a critical part of your early success . . . until it isn't. I'm not going to lie to you—there's no easy answer when dealing with these situations. There's no hard-and-fast rule that says, "Two years in, you need to replace your generalists with specialists!" or "Once you've hit $1 million in revenue, bring in a COO!" It all depends on your company, your growth, and your vision—as well as your Betty's skill set, emotional intelligence, and career goals. There's a lot of moving parts here, and there's no one-size-fits-all solution. Definitely more art than science!

As we saw with Tom, companies will usually need to bring in specialists to lead the various functional areas of the business. For first-timers, it might take a bit longer to realize that, but most get there eventually.

Hiring specialists offers a few key advantages beyond the obvious, "They know what they're doing!" angle. First off, you can hire someone who has critical experience working in a company your size, in your industry, or at your pace of growth. I've talked a lot about the need to add a few key leaders who've got the experience needed to help you reach your goals. But here, I'm talking pretty early in the game, so you're not ready to bring in a heavy hitter just yet. Hiring functional specialists is your opportunity to add people to the team with insight and experience to improve the prototypes Betty built, taking additional steps to make the company better and stronger.

Adding experience gives you the opportunity to start professionalizing your team, putting pieces in place for future growth. You're confident that Bounce-Around Betty will always figure things out—but what if your team didn't have to "figure it out" and already knew what to do? Betty was great on the phone with early customers, but she's not the right person to design and build the customer service engine, including processes, tools, and the team you need for future growth.

Bounce-Around Betty is such an important employee for entrepreneurial companies, partially because you can't hire all the specialists you may want all at once, and partially because you simply can't predict every area of need before you need it. She fills a critical role at a critical time! Tom's example above is fairly common. He prioritized the e-commerce engine, then as soon as he could afford to hire someone to improve upon Betty's work, he did. He then asked her to tackle his next challenges—fulfillment, then customer service, then accounting, and so on. You get the picture.

It's great that Betty is willing to take on whatever

challenge is next, especially something else she knows nothing about. She's able to learn on the fly and do "good enough," like she always has. But eventually you'll reach a point where "good enough" just isn't, well, good enough. Betty's best asset has become a liability. She's a Swiss Army knife, and the company now needs a scalpel.

When Betty Goes Bad

For a slightly different twist on this near-universal challenge, let me tell you about a good friend of mine who runs a very successful professional services firm in Florida. Three friends got together and started the company ten years prior. Early on, the three of them were partners and split duties, doing whatever needed to be done to the best of their abilities. Tonya, Jim, and Bernie each did a little bit of everything and each "bounced around" to whatever needed doing next.

Tonya was the majority owner and was also the visionary leader. She led the firm and served as managing partner. Jim was a strong subject-matter expert and immersed himself in client service and management of key accounts. But Bernie never really grew beyond the generalist phase. He wasn't as strong as Tonya and Jim and didn't have an obvious role, so he kept bouncing around for a lot longer than he should have. He did his best in whatever role he was asked to perform. But as the company grew, it became apparent that his best wasn't good enough. So, he bounced and bounced.

This case is a bit unusual because Bernie was a partner and co-founder of the business, so he wanted a leadership role like Tonya and Jim had. When the company grew to the point of needing a sales leader or human resources leader, Bernie wanted those roles. But he wasn't qualified to lead those teams—and to be honest, he wasn't really qualified to be a "leader" at all.

As Bernie bounced from one leadership role to another, Tonya spent time fixing whatever mess he left behind. Most of the team HATED working for Bernie as he tried to "figure it out." They were more talented than him, they knew what they were doing, and he only got in the way. But they didn't feel like they could tell Bernie he was wrong or go over his head because he was a partner.

At one point, Bernie needed to add several new hires to the marketing team he was leading. In chapter 9 I talk about B-players hiring C-players (they definitely don't hire A-players!). Well, Bernie was no different. He shied away from A-players or candidates who wanted to build a world-class marketing department. He was insecure, and this was how he protected himself.

This example is obviously an egregious one. Normally your Betty won't be a partner, so you won't feel as constrained as Tonya did. But in this case, her Betty is still bouncing around to various departments and leadership roles. He won't accept a lesser position, and Tonya and Jim are too loyal to force the issue, even though doing so would help the business tremendously. To be honest, this issue has really harmed Tonya's status as the leader of the company. Why? Because almost every other employee sees the same issues with this arrangement that you probably do!

From Bouncing Around to Growing Professionally

In most cases, Betty's a good employee who doesn't need to leave just because you need more specialists. She's a valuable member of the team and can continue adding value if she's in the right role.

Much of what happens with Betty will depend on how you approach the situation. As usual, it also depends on the personalities, expectations, and egos involved. If you demote Betty to assistant to the new VP of Sales without giving her a heads-up—yeah, that'll piss her off. But do it right, and you can put Betty AND your company in a great position to succeed.

Hopefully you now realize that you can't solve this problem by giving Betty whatever role she wants. However, if most of your leadership team has proven, relevant experience and has a mentor mindset, and Betty is willing and able to learn under their tutelage, then she's probably someone you can invest in.

Identify the role that plays best to Betty's strengths and allows her to grow professionally, but also fuels the company's growth goals. That's easier said than done and may require some soul-searching and tough conversations.

If your relationship with Betty has a foundation of trust and open communication, you should be able to approach her and discuss the situation. Be honest with her. Her knack for figuring things out has been a great asset, but a different skill set is needed now. You need leaders who have skins on the wall. Sure, you want to help develop her skills so she can grow professionally—AND you need her to help position the company to achieve its goals.

I've had a few of these conversations. When I've made it clear that I'm new to this too, it helps "Betty" understand. The reason you're adding proven leaders to the leadership team is because YOU DON'T WANT TO LEARN EVERYTHING THE HARD WAY. Betty should understand this; after all, you've been through a lot together!

Sometimes, she'll push back. She thinks she's ready to lead marketing because of everything she did to develop the brand. She argues that she knows the company better than anyone. She can do this! But remember, your goal isn't to make her happy. Your goal is to professionalize your organization to grow beyond anything Betty—or you—has previously experienced. Explain this to her and make sure she knows that her professional growth is also important to you. Tell her your plan to bring in someone to mentor her to become a future leader with your company or elsewhere. If she's humble and values the opportunity, she'll jump at the chance to learn under a next-level leader.

If you're anything like me, it's hard to have these conversations. More often than I care to admit, I've given in to Betty and given her whatever position she wanted. But trust me, you're not doing her any favors by putting her in a position to fail.

If you find yourself struggling with situations like this, consider bringing in another set of eyes. Have your mentor or coach assess your Betty situation and give you their perspective. This helps to remove your personal feelings from the equation.

Remember, your goal isn't to promote Betty until she

fails miserably. You want to do what's best for the company and ideally find the right spot for her to grow. This balance can be tricky, but with the right approach and the right Betty, it can be found! Check out Intermission I for more ideas on how to deal with your own Betty situation.

INTERMISSION I

ASSESSING YOUR TEAM

"People are not your most important asset. The right people are."

– **Jim Collins** in *Good to Great*[2]

What do you do when you think you've outgrown long-term, legacy members of your team? Legacy employees like Mike, Bounce-Around Betty, Right-Hand Rita, and others, who were once key members of your band of misfits. They helped you scrap and claw your way from startup to success. But where do they fit in now that you're professionalizing your team, and adding key leaders who've done this before? Or how do you know if you've simply made a bad hire?

You may also be asking how you're supposed to identify talented future leaders on your team. Or "how do I know when to 'demote' someone by putting them back into an individual contributor role or cut my losses altogether?" This intermission will help you answer those questions and more. Let's jump right in!

Assess Your Team

Most entrepreneurs hire reactively. It may work for some of you, but for the vast majority of us, that's how we end up with people problems. I think there're at least three important things you can do at this stage of growth to build a great team. Before you even begin recruiting, you should: (1) know where your company's headed; (2) know the key initiatives that will drive that growth; and (3) assess your existing team against those initiatives.

"Where I'm headed?" But I need help now!

That's right. The first step in assessing your team and how they fit in, is to know where you're going. Where do you want your business to be in three to five years? Your vision for the company will impact your team's hiring needs. Let's say you're planning to grow revenue from $10 to $25 million in the next two to three years; how do you plan to do that? Maybe you're going to open a new office, launch a new product, or buy a competitor.

Your answer to that question will help determine the talent you'll need to achieve your goals. For example, if you're going to triple revenue by simply selling more, you'll likely need an experienced sales leader to build the infrastructure to scale that department. Harry the Hustler is probably not the best fit to build that next-level infrastructure.

But first things first. In order to determine whether your team has what it takes to get you "there," you first need to know where "there" is. No one has a crystal ball, and this isn't a lesson in predicting the future, but you should have an idea that's directionally accurate. If you don't, you'll be continually frustrated on the hiring front. Like Yogi Berra said, "If you don't know where you're going, you might wind up someplace else."

I have some goals in mind, but how do I know if my team can do it?

This is honestly some of the hardest stuff I cover with clients. Even in my own story, which you'll learn later in this book, I had trouble identifying which team members were diamonds in the rough and which were just rough! It's not easy—especially when it comes to legacy employees you've come to know and love from your time together in the trenches.

I learned that there's no way to just "know" who will make it long term. You can lose a ton of sleep over it, but you're probably not going to wake up one morning and know that Mike is the weakest link, for example.

But in my nearly three decades working with high-growth, entrepreneurial companies, I've developed a few key questions you can ask yourself to identify the key players and the weak links on your team. It's not an exact science (nothing ever is!), but this will help you validate your gut feeling or provide some clarity. These questions originated with middle-market gurus like Gino Wickman, Verne Harnish, Jim Collins, and Brad Smart (among others), and they've been honed in hundreds of HireBetter client sessions over the years. They work!

As you read these questions, think about each member of your team: legacy employees, new hires—it doesn't really matter. I've included examples of each here, in brackets. When you start assessing your team based on these simple questions—and answer them honestly—you'll gain clarity.

#1 Knowing today what you know about your organization and where you're going, would you enthusiastically rehire [Mike] for his current role?

I believe this is the single most important question you can ask yourself about every member of the team. Think about how this question can inform your decision-making moving forward. With someone like Mike, for example, you'd be lying to yourself if you said, "Yes! I would enthusiastically rehire Mike as my CFO!" Now, this doesn't mean Mike needs to go, but he's probably not the strategic CFO you need for this next stage of growth.

#2 Does [Harry] have the skills, experience, and tools to get us to the next level, however we choose to define that?

This one's a little more nuanced than #1. Harry the Hustler may have the passion and skills, but does he have the experience required to get you there? If not, you may want to pair him with a coach or advisor who has that experience. Otherwise, the road to where you're going is going to be filled with a lot of potholes.

And in Harry's case, once you promote him to sales leader, you've not only lost your #1 salesman, you're also handing the reins to someone who has never built a sales organization or managed a team of salespeople. You're probably setting him (and them) up for failure.

#3 What if I had a team of [Bettys]? How strong would we be?

This question can help you check your gut, since it's a hypothetical exercise and will evoke an emotional reaction. If you get a sinking feeling thinking about a team of Bounce-Around Bettys, then that's a pretty good indicator for how you feel about Betty.

#4 What if [Ralph] came into my office and quit tomorrow morning. How would I feel?

Another good, gut feeling question. If reading that question made you panic and start thinking about ways to stop him from quitting, that MAY be your answer. However, don't confuse a short-term pain in the ass with the right longer-term answer. If you're anything like me, you hate the thought of dealing with any employee turnover.

Losing Ralph may still be the right answer, but it'll suck in the short term. If you paused for a moment and thought *Damn, that would make life MUCH easier!* that's probably your answer.

So many questions! Now what?

Here's the fun part. If your answers were generally positive, this next section will help you with next steps to further develop those employees. If your answers were negative—something like, "Yep, Paul sucks!" all the way to, "I sure don't want a team filled with Ritas"—then feel free to skip ahead to the "When Things Go Wrong" section!

The Positives

When you've got an employee who's an A-player in their current role, you want to keep them, and you want to fuel their motivation! But how do you keep them energized without promoting them too far, turning your A-player into a future problem? It's a balancing act. An employee kicking ass in their current role doesn't necessarily translate if overpromoted. Overpromotion is a sure way to turn today's heroes into tomorrow's problems.

Harry the Hustler, for example, is a rockstar salesman. You leaned on him as your company grew from idea to reality. But Harry's sales acumen doesn't mean he's got the experience or skills to build a scalable sales process, complete with a team of junior Harrys!

How do I know if Harry, or any other great employee, is right for a next-level leadership role?

The first step, again, is to know your goals. Then design an ideal candidate profile, or blueprint, for the position you're creating. Map out the skills and experience you'll need BEFORE you consider current employees. If you want to get there faster and with fewer lessons learned in the School of Hard Knocks, then you'll be looking for experience scaling a high-growth, entrepreneurial company. It's not about want-to, it's about know-how! This exercise can demonstrate that while you may love your employees in their current roles, they don't have what you need next. As Denzel Washington says in *Training Day*, "This shit's chess, it ain't checkers!"[3]

Once you've determined that you should look outside for this new role, the hard part begins. And it's definitely an art. Sit down with the employee and be open and honest about the new role. Explain how different the duties and expectations are from what they've been doing. Depending on the role, it can be easy. For Harry, as an example, explain that "sales leader" is less entrepreneurial and more operational. Instead of pounding the pavement making sales, he'd be installing a system to track sales. Instead of earning commission, he'd be paid a base salary. For many stud salespeople, the lack of commission might be enough for them to self-select out!

What if my employee WANTS the promotion?

When you sit down with them, make sure you're getting to the heart of the matter. What is it they actually want?

Everyone wants to be rewarded for their efforts, especially when they know they're a huge part of what got you to where you are today!

In most cases, the employee will want to feel like they're "moving up"—whether that's in title, prestige, equity, or compensation. The company is growing, in large part on the backs of folks like Mike, Harry, and Rita. It's only natural for them to want to grow with the company. Listen carefully to what they say, because it'll make a huge difference in how you handle the situation.

If they want a promotion simply because they want more money, well, that's not enough reason for you. And in some cases, the promotion may not mean more money! This is probably true for Harry, since he's a commission-based individual contributor. That's important for these guys and gals to know when having these discussions.

It's also important to point out that, while they're expected to perform at high levels, there probably won't be many big, short-term financial incentives baked in. Sure, they might earn more equity or longer-term incentives based on growth, but Harry probably loves the thrill of earning an immediate 5 percent commission on every sale he makes!

If it's just about the title and perceived prestige that comes with a promotion, there are other ways to make that happen. For example, one founder friend promoted her main salesperson to "partner" when facing this situation. I've seen title changes used effectively when cash was short. The title was elevated but the duties remained the same. To quote almost every entrepreneur ever, "Titles are cheap!" There's a difference between job titles and job duties.

Be careful though. Title inflation is real and may cause issues down the road. It's hard to go out and recruit a kickass chief operating officer, for example, if Bounce-Around Betty holds that title.

Investing in Your Employees

What do I do—promote them?

In some cases, the right move may be to promote your employee, with the caveat that you will also bring in an interim or fractional leader in that position to lead and teach them the ropes. When targeting this person, you'll want to prioritize mentorship and relevant experience. Investing in an executive coach for them may also be a good move.

Bringing in a coach or mentor demonstrates to your employee that you're invested in their professional growth, and you want to help them become the leader you know they can be. Make sure you communicate this up front and keep up that communication! Remind them that you're investing in their future.

For those of you thinking, *Hell, I'll mentor them; they look up to me*, I would discourage this approach. I'm going to assume that for most functional roles, entrepreneurs don't have the skills, experience, or time necessary to mentor them. Invest in them and enhance their chances for success by bringing in someone from the outside to take on this mentorship role.

So I'm supposed to tell them, "I believe in you, but not enough to promote you." How do I do that?

Throughout every step of this process, you've got to manage expectations and feelings—AND run a business. As always, I encourage you to be open and honest! Don't make promises you may not be able to keep. "I'm not sure this is the right fit for you or for us, but we'll train you to help us decide" is an honest statement. Be careful not to dangle carrots they can never catch!

This open and honest approach to workplace relationships is hard but worth it in the long run. Your employees will trust you to shoot straight with them and will believe you when you say you're not sure. Remind them that this is the first time YOU are going through this as well. You know you need to surround yourself with relevant experience. Tell them you want them to gain experience so they can lead in the future—whether it's with your company or another.

Egos might be bruised, but with honesty and good communication, great employees will trust that you're making the best decisions for all involved.

When Things Go Wrong

Let's talk about one of the hardest things about being an entrepreneur. What do we do when people aren't working out—or we're not sure if they're going to work out? Forget about promoting Harry the Hustler, you've got major concerns about Right-Hand Rita, and you may need to fire Pipeline Paul. People issues are the worst! They're not easy for any of us.

What are my options?

With problem employees, you usually have three options: (1) coach them into the leader you need them to be; (2) move them into a different role; or (3) terminate their employment.

The option you choose depends on a number of variables that are impossible for me to know from afar. But remember that if your team—especially your leadership team—isn't getting the job done, YOU are ultimately responsible. You can't sit idle while the company flounders. No matter what decision you make, it's your decision. No one can make it for you. The buck stops with you.

Alright then, I guess I need to fire some people.

Wait a second! Before we go off and fire people, there are some important things to consider. For certain roles, I encourage you to consult with an employment attorney. There are protected employment classes that make it harder to part ways. In other cases, the employee may have access to sensitive company data you need to protect (especially if he or she could be a vindictive a-hole!), or you may simply need to be sure your i's are dotted and your t's are crossed.

It's also essential to ask yourself some important questions, especially with legacy employees you feel loyal to:

1) **Are there other ways he or she can contribute to the business?**
Smart, talented, well-connected, and well-respected people can often contribute to entrepreneurial companies in a variety of ways: maybe not in their current roles, but perhaps somewhere else in the organization. Just be careful. After all, we don't want Resume Ralph to turn into Bounce-Around Betty! Maybe there's a part-time consulting or commission-based sales position, or simply an individual contributor role that may be a fit for them.

2) **Is he or she coachable or salvageable?**
In certain cases, you might be just a mentor away from a future leader. Maybe Techno Tim needs an executive coach for help leading a team, or Bounce-Around Betty just needs a mentor to learn management skills. Consider investing in members of your team who have the skills, capabilities, and drive to become the leader you need.

However, don't bring in a coach as a way to kick the can down the road, simply because you don't want to make the tough call now. You don't need any pet projects. I can't tell you how many times I've seen entrepreneurs take on a "good person" who's struggling and try to make him or her successful. I call it the stray dog theory—and it rarely works! You're growing too fast, and your team is already stretched thin. They don't need any doomed projects to keep them busy.

Is it time to terminate?

If your gut's telling you it's time, your gut is probably right. It may be time to consider letting them go. Let's start with the two things you shouldn't do: 1) overreact, or 2) nothing. You can't panic in these situations. But you also can't stick your head in the sand and hope it goes away.

If you're not sure and you feel like you need some validation, there are a few ways to accomplish that. The most common mistake, and the one I caution clients about the most, is to ask your team what they think.

Remember that feedback from the team can be tricky. On one hand, maybe the problem employee is a slimeball who treats people like crap and his only concern is his bonus. But on the other hand, maybe he's frustrating the legacy team simply because they liked the old way of doing things. Now they're being held accountable, and change is disconcerting to them! When you bring in a next-level leader to professionalize your company, by definition they'll do things differently than before—which is usually a good thing!

Having said that, discussions with key team members you trust to be objective can provide good data points. Just make sure your questions don't come across as a witch hunt. Once the legacy team smells blood in the water, the ensuing feeding frenzy isn't likely to provide much clarity for anybody.

Is there some other way to get a second opinion?

The most effective second opinion, in my experience, is to identify a trusted third party to assess the situation. I personally invited a YPO Forum buddy, an operational guru, to step in and give me the straight poop when HireBetter was having challenges back in 2015. I've seen other leaders have success asking advisors, consultants, or trusted friends for second opinions as well.

I don't want any alarm bells ringing. How can I be discreet about this?

In some situations, you can be upfront with your employee and tell him why you're assessing his or her performance, but that's not the norm. If you aren't sure what (or who) is causing the problems, it's probably best to proceed with caution. If you're concerned about ruffling feathers, blame the board, the bank, or even an investor as a scapegoat.

As a side note, I've found folks like Techno Tim to be especially defensive in the face of scrutiny. And the more defensive he is, the greater the probability that he's the problem. People get defensive when backed into a corner. When that happens, it's important to move quickly, because he may try to take you down with him, if given the opportunity!

I've carefully considered the information available . . . and it's time to fire away!

Time to put your big-boy or big-girl pants on! Terminating someone isn't pleasant. No one likes to do it. But it's not something you can outsource, and you definitely can't hide from it. Tackle the problem head-on. Whatever you do, don't sit idle. If you let the situation go on too long, your company could suffer.

If the ultimate answer is that you need to remove and replace—just f-ing do it (once you consult with your HR counsel). Don't worry about hurt feelings or difficult conversations. You're making your business stronger! And your team will probably ask, "What took you so long?"

In the Techno Tim chapter you'll meet Jeff. In his case, inaction was a big part of his company's failure. The longer the wound festered, the more infected it became. And when a bad "leader" is in power, you're usually the last to know. Their team won't feel comfortable talking to you about issues while he's there, but once he's gone—damn, do those floodgates open!

Wish me luck?

Again, firing someone, especially a legacy employee you actually like, is not pleasant. Just remember: you're making the best decision you can for your company. The most critical move you can make is to ACT. Let it fester too long and it'll only get worse!

"Letting go of longtime employees is pure agony. We're talking about lifelong friends, the people who followed you into the business when nobody else believed in it. You wouldn't be here without them. But for most entrepreneurs, there comes a time when you realize you've simply outgrown a key lieutenant."

– **Doug Tatum,** author of *No Man's Land*

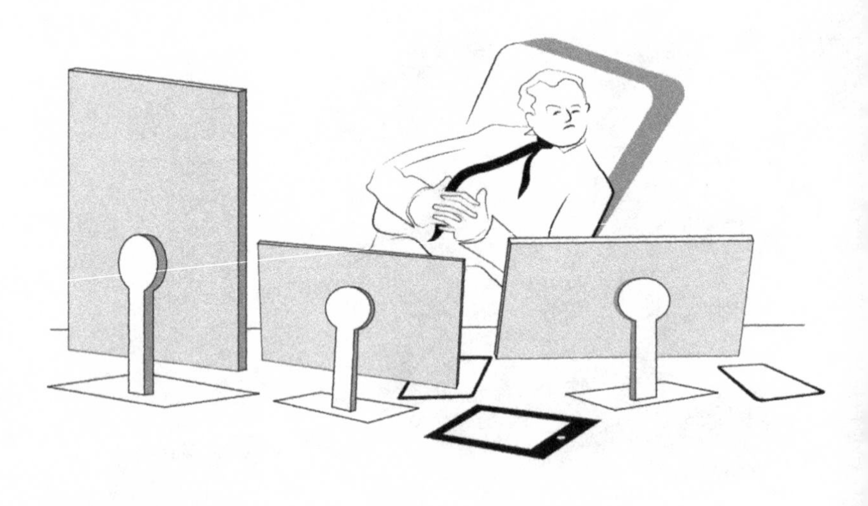

06

TECHNO TIM

THE SMARTEST GUY IN THE ROOM

"The irony about hiring a brilliant jerk is that you immediately lose most of the good ideas from the rest of the team. They shut down when a know-it-all shows up. After making this mistake multiple times, I've learned that the damage to the team is never worth one person's supposed genius."

– **Suzi Sosa,** CEO and Co-Founder, Verb

For many entrepreneurial companies, their success relies on the proficiency of one or two strong individuals in the technical aspects of the business. Maybe it's software development, artificial intelligence, or product development, or maybe it's subject matter expertise in some form of accounting, engineering, or construction design. Bottom line is that a technical leader occupies a critical role—probably the most important role in the early stages of growth.

But expertise doesn't make someone a great team player. While I've been around many successful tech startups, I've also seen many entrepreneurs struggle with prima donnas: guys who weren't shy about letting you know they were the smartest person in the room. I've seen tech leaders who range from amazingly egotistical and hard to work with, all the way to maniacal and diabolical. I've seen poor communicators and others who surround themselves with yes-men. And I've seen many projects fall behind and go over budget because leaders were afraid to admit they made a mistake.

If any of this resonates, read on. This chapter focuses on Tim as a technology subject matter expert (SME), but you can probably substitute other technical gurus or SMEs in most of the stories.

The Entrepreneur

Most of the successful entrepreneurs I know aren't true "tech guys." Sure, they know enough to be dangerous and they got the business started, but they need those uber technical whizzes around them to make the business truly successful.

I'm looking in the mirror when I say this: many entrepreneurs are skilled in a lot of different areas and soft skills, but we often can't even figure out our damn Wi-Fi network at home, let alone design and produce innovative technology. Hell, some of my founder buddies may even be knowledgeable about the latest technological advances, trends, and forecasts. But even the entrepreneurs who stay up to date on the latest and greatest usually don't remain the most technical.

Techno Tim

Techno Tim is WICKED smart: as in, smartest guy in the room and not afraid to let you know it smart; as in, talks for hours and hours about stuff you only sort of understand smart. Not only does he talk the talk, but he seems to REALLY get it! He can take your idea, break it down to the nuts and bolts, and put it back together again in the course of a conversation.

Entrepreneurial CEOs look to guys like Techno Tim all the time. Sure, you came up with a brilliant and innovative idea, but let's face the facts. You have a vision for the product or service; you know how to sell and how to lead. But at the end of the day, you have no f-ing clue how to actually develop, test, and build a scalable product! You need someone you can count on to develop the technology platform, complete with all the bells and whistles you imagined. You need someone with the technological expertise to get your idea into the hands of consumers.

You know this is a gap for your young company. But this point is beaten home through various discussions with mentors and investors. "Who's your CTO?" they ask. "Who's the tech leader who's going to oversee product development?"

You've been reaching out to your network, looking for a stud. An investor introduces you to Techno Tim, and you're blown away. He's the #2 tech guy at a very successful company in town. But in his mind, he basically does the job of the #1 guy—and they're missing out on a real opportunity. Sure, the company has done well, "but they could be so much better if they'd just listen to me," he says. He wows you with his knowledge of tech stacks, coding, and the future of open source, along with other techspeak you vaguely understand. He knows all the newest and hottest technologies. In fact, he JUST got back from a mega conference the industry is buzzing about.

If you've ever worked for, worked with, or been around entrepreneurial companies that require technical expertise, you recognize this conversation: the one where you absolutely fall in love with Techno Tim, or at least the concept of Techno Tim. You don't know how you'll succeed without him. He's eager to showcase his brilliance for the right company, and you need a genius to complete your team. Tim's a perfect fit! He's a tech guru, he's got a great resume—and he was referred by an investor you trust (more on that later). You've probably convinced yourself that passing on Tim would be a huge mistake—as bad as the Trailblazers passing on Michael Jordan in the '84 draft!

You start to imagine what you can do with Tim on the team. The sky's the limit! Investors love the promise of your technology. Pair that with Tim's resume, and you're on your way! Most importantly, Tim was recommended by a trusted investor, for heaven's sake. And at this time in your company's lifecycle, referrals carry a TON of weight. What could go wrong? You're following the unicorn playbook: venture capital, world-class team, working prototype, and top-notch customer logos as early adopters. The only question is whether you'll sell the company to private equity or go public.

What Could Go Wrong?

You make the seemingly obvious choice to bring Techno Tim on board, and things start out great. He points out that the code your legacy team developed wasn't up to snuff; "It'll never scale and support the type of growth we want," he says. He plans to start by taking the time to "fix it, make it right." You're so relieved, because without Tim, you wouldn't have known until it was too late!

So, you leave Tim to do his work; he IS the tech whiz, after all. Meanwhile, you focus on raising the money you'll need to make this happen and wowing early-adopter customers with the promise of your solution. You attack your role with energy and vigor. Your dreams are coming true! Tim looks good for the dog and pony show. His resume impresses the local venture capital firms, and he certainly talks the talk.

But behind the scenes, things aren't going so well. While Tim is very smart, it takes teamwork to make the dream work. Remember how I said Tim likes to be the smartest guy in the room? Turns out that's not a good thing. He doesn't like to be challenged. He needs to be THE guy. At every opportunity, he reminds you how smart he is and how most everyone else, well . . . isn't. Tim surrounds himself with people who agree with him all the time, unwittingly hiring a team of B- and C-players who are afraid to challenge him.

The cracks start to show a few months in . . . subtle at first. When you reflect back on your experience, you realize you should have asked more questions early on. For example, the weekly management team meetings turned into a what-will-the-excuse-be-this-week exercise. At first, Tim was spending a lot of time talking about how the current technology would never scale and he would have to re-do a lot of what was previously built. It all made sense to you at the time (and it may have been true). After all, you brought in an expert to build this thing right.

Tim would regale the team with the latest open-source technology he's planning to use to fix one issue or another. He always wants to dabble in the new whizbang technologies out there. In retrospect, you suspect that he was probably just padding his resume or building relationships with key software and hardware vendors to further his career.

Deadlines were slipping and he was way over budget. "Be patient, we're doing something that's never been done before," he would say. Or my favorite, as the type of condescending things typical Techno Tims often say, "Kurt, you just don't understand! This is a complicated problem we're trying to solve." At some point you just want to punch Tim in the nose!

What you don't know is that Tim is creating manual overrides to cover up the bigger problems with his team's work. The issue goes deeper than you think. But what you do know is that the excuses for why things aren't on schedule are becoming more vociferous. He's definitely an A-player in the excuse department! The previous code had bigger issues than he thought, or the software vendor is an idiot, or "the board is demanding things that just aren't possible on such a short timeline," or perhaps his team is "just a bunch of whiny millennials."

Tim knows you're not sure whether he's full of shit or

not. You're not a tech guy. He knows he has a long leash, and he can continue talking in circles to keep you satisfied. Whatever the excuse, Tim constantly reminds you how hard his job is to do—and by extension, reminds you how lost you'd be without him. You're frustrated, but at the same time you're scared you might lose him. And then you'd have nowhere to turn. That may be true . . . or you may be better off without him.

The pressure is building on you every day. The board and your investors (and your exec team!) are starting to doubt you as a leader. What can you do? I've seen some clients and friends successfully bring in outside experts to poke around and assess the situation. If you choose to go that route with your Techno Tim, proceed with caution! As the smartest person in the room, he doesn't like to be questioned. If he gets the sense that you're messing around in his kitchen, he'll feel threatened and honestly might blow up on you. He'll get even more defensive and make your life a living hell. That doesn't mean you shouldn't do it; it just means you should have a plan.

You may feel like you can't live without Tim, but the truth is, you can! There are a few options for what to do with a Techno Tim before it's too late, and we'll get to those later. Just know that you'll eventually reach a point where it IS too late. When the project looks like it will never get done or your board or investors lose faith in you, your investors will start to pull out. Sometimes, Tim will quit when he sees the writing on the wall. He doesn't want to go down with the ship. (Come to think of it, did you ever independently verify why he left his last job?) At some point, whether you expose the issue, or the shit just naturally hits the fan, the leak in the *Titanic* will be too large for the mop pails to bail out. And everything will come crashing down on Tim—and on you.

Real-World Example

I've got a ton of real-life Techno Tim stories, and I'm sure you do too. Here's just one example.

My friend Jeff founded an e-commerce company during the dotcom heydays, with little more than a great idea, some top-notch connections, and some well-worded scribbles on the back of a napkin. Without disclosing too much, his idea to partner with high-traffic websites and run their online e-commerce stores was novel at the time and well-received. He validated his idea with industry leaders and successfully circled up some early-stage investment capital to get the company off the ground.

But while Jeff was the idea man and had a clear vision for what he wanted the company to be, he wasn't the tech whiz who was going to design and implement his brilliant idea. He knew he needed one, a chief technology officer, a technology partner.

One of Jeff's board members and largest investors referred him to Tim. Jeff was not about to piss off his largest investor, so they met—and Jeff was blown away. Tim was very impressive and talked a great game. He had spent the previous fourteen years at a large and very successful organization, managing a large team. His team ran everything from tech support for over 1,000 desktops to the company's enterprise resource planning (ERP) system. He had even overseen the design of the company's nascent e-commerce engine. Dotcom mania was sweeping the country, Tim was eager to step out and punch the "tech startup" lottery ticket, and he believed in Jeff's idea.

Beyond his on-paper experience, Tim dazzled Jeff with his brilliance, especially when it came to new tech. He seemed to understand cutting-edge technologies better than anyone. He swept Jeff away, and it didn't take long for Jeff to fall in love with him and offer him the job. He needed someone to leverage these new technologies and turn his idea into a reality, and Tim sure seemed to fit the bill.

Jeff placed complete trust in Tim to develop the technology infrastructure while he focused on selling his vision to key customers and strategic partners. The initial plan was to develop a working prototype and win some name-brand early adopters through Jeff's relationships. Then they would show off these early wins to alliance partners, build some marketplace buzz, and raise big-time venture capital ahead of the inevitable IPO and check-cashing frenzy.

Unfortunately, things didn't go as planned. The tech always seemed to be behind schedule and over budget—not a great combo! Monday management meetings began to feel like *Groundhog Day* for Jeff (without the Andie MacDowell part, of course). Early on, Tim would rave about the latest and greatest shiny-object tech he was considering buying or implementing, but he never seemed to get things across the finish line.

When Jeff pressed for answers, Tim was well-armed with excuses, ranging from "I have a new team" or "this has never been done before/new technology is complicated" to "these things take time." Or my favorite, "there were some bugs in the software. We're fixing them, but I want it to be perfect before I show it off to you."

Like many of the other versions of himself, this Techno Tim considered himself to be the smartest person in the room. Well, when someone like that is in charge of hiring a team, that's a self-fulfilling prophecy. In this case, Jeff empowered Tim, giving him complete control over the makeup of his team. And while Tim probably didn't set out to hire a team of B- and C-players, he definitely gravitated toward people who agreed with him. Some might say he didn't want anyone who would challenge his place on the throne, but I believe he simply liked it when people kissed his ass. And this played out in interviews. If you were into his ego, his ideas, or his vision for cutting-edge tech, then you passed. If not, you probably just "weren't a culture fit" or otherwise didn't make the cut.

Without opposing viewpoints on the team, anyone willing (or able?) to challenge Tim, or even anyone to simply remind him of the task at hand, it didn't take long for tiny cracks to develop and quickly become gaping holes. "It will be done next week" became next month, which inevitably got pushed out—again and again. As Jeff grew increasingly frustrated, Tim placed more and more blame on others. First it was the software, then the third-party development firm he outsourced much of the work to, then "the incompetent team I had to hire on such a small budget." By the end, everything that came out of Tim's mouth was some form of "It's not me, it's them."

When you build a house of cards around yourself, as Tim did, the only question is WHEN it will come tumbling down, not if. Through this process, Jeff learned valuable lessons about hiring, but he probably picked up a "real-life MBA" in managing his team and holding people accountable, which are things most entrepreneurs tend to struggle with.

Unfortunately, these lessons were learned the hard way for Jeff. In the end, all the delays hurt his chances to woo his next round of investors, crippling the company's chances. When the economy took a downturn, it didn't take long for the company to go under as well. In fairness, even with working tech, the company probably would've struggled in the downturn, but Techno Tim certainly didn't help its chances!

What Can You Do about Techno Tim?

If you find yourself with a Techno Tim on your hands, you have a number of options. Let me preface by saying that you're not always right. And even though you're a successful entrepreneur, your gut isn't always right, either. What I mean by that is you probably want to get a second opinion before you fire off half-cocked, especially with such a critical role. But you do need to recognize that you have a problem; dig in to see how real or how deep the issue is. Having said that, in Intermission I included a number of things for you to consider and options to weigh in dealing with Tim. And in Intermission II, beginning on page 135, I've provided some tips on avoiding Techno Tim in the first place. Good luck!

OUT OF
OFFICE
#1
GRANDPA
again

07

RESUME RALPH

HE LOOKED **SO** GOOD ON PAPER

"Building a company for scale is a balance. Eventually, founder-CEOs need to add leaders who have larger company experience (building steady processes and defined procedures)—but who are also comfortable building in the steady-state "chaos" of a startup. As such, founders should identify experienced leaders who can thrive in an ever-changing environment and bring order to chaos."

– **Paul Hedrick,** Founder & CEO, Tecovas

Entrepreneurial companies are exciting, demanding, chaotic, rewarding, and frenetic—in short, a thing of beauty. But they're not for everyone. Along your journey, you'll encounter key inflection points where you get to make decisions about maintaining status quo or investing in [fill-in-the-blank] to put your company over the top.

One of those decisions will involve moving from generalists to specialists on your team. Instead of the all-hands-on-deck approach that got you to this point, it's time to build out departments and make key hires to lead them. If you want to scale your company, you're going to have to make some changes: strategic moves that, as you might expect, can be a jolt to the system.

As for you, you're doing your best to juggle all the balls in the air, but you're struggling to keep up, as well. And while you love to roll up your sleeves, get your hands dirty, and make things happen, you're very aware that you need to be "working ON your business and not IN your business," as the saying goes. You know you should be thinking about how to grow your company from $5 million to $20 million, not who's going to take out the trash today! Easier said than done.

You're tired. You've been at this a long time, and you just want a silver bullet. Someone who can run this for you. Maybe it's a VP or chief revenue officer to run sales. Maybe you want to hand over product development or operations. Many of you will aim even higher—a chief operating officer, EOS Integrator, or even president or CEO.[4] The title doesn't really matter—you just want a proven, professional, experienced leader to shoulder the heavy load and free you up to focus on things you're good at, and that you enjoy!

This is where I've seen many of my entrepreneurial clients, and friends—including myself—make key, unlocking moves. And it's also where I've seen a number of them make critical mistakes. Oftentimes, we fall in love with the resume of a potential key hire and project our hopes and dreams on them as our white knight. We definitely put on our rose-colored glasses.

Enter Resume Ralph, whose background seemed too good to be true—and it was.

Ralph looked GREAT on paper. In his twenty-five-year career, he had done it all! Twenty years with a big-name Fortune 500 company and five years with businesses closer to yours in size—most in your industry and all apparently successful. You can't believe your luck; this guy is amazing! You bring him in without doing much due diligence, because it seems like such a no-brainer.

Turns out Ralph is full of shit. He's ridden coattails since he left the big company, and any success was in spite of him rather than because of him. Ralph talks a good game and puts together a mean PowerPoint, but the only chance he'll be successful is if he can hire great people who do his job for him—in addition to their own. Alas, you can't afford someone in an ivory tower just directing traffic, so Ralph fails miserably. Any of this sound familiar? If so, keep reading about Resume Ralph.

The Entrepreneur

When entrepreneurs begin looking for help at the top, we often think big: "I need someone who can help me run the show . . . but ideally someone who can sell too!" You might be thinking about the need to raise capital, business development needs, or relationships you don't have or simply haven't had the time or energy to build.

One mistake I've seen entrepreneurs make time and again is the quest for a unicorn: the Rockstar leader, a builder of teams who has key industry contacts and amazing BizDev skills, is a subject-matter expert, a sought-after speaker, a lover of the arts, and on and on. Oh, and is willing to work for peanuts. My friends, unicorns don't exist!

The other common mistake is getting wooed by that

mythical person. In the darkness, you see someone who can be that game-changer, who can turn things around overnight! You say something like, "We've been trying to sell software to HP for years, and this guy's an HP vet. Maybe he's our next sales leader!" or "We need someone who knows how things work at Conagra. I think they'll buy us!" or "I just want someone to hand the keys to. I'm tired and I want to focus on the product." But the truth is, there's no shortcut to building the right team to set you up for rocket ship growth.

While wanting qualities like these in a new leader is perfectly natural, they're not the be-all, end-all. Getting tunnel vision about a hypothetical relationship, a future deal, or yes, a unicorn, is a GREAT way to get burned. That's how you end up with Resume Ralph.

Who Is Resume Ralph?

Whether you put out feelers to your network, work with a recruiter, or advertise the job far and wide, you'll likely end up with a few candidates that look great on paper. But one definitely stands out. Ralph went to the right school, he had a long and storied career at a name brand Fortune 500 company, and he's spent the last five years in your industry. He's perfect, right?

You can't believe your luck. Ralph will open so many doors just by walking into the office! He'll bring key relationships and oodles of experience. His resume is a siren song. It lays out everything you think you want and more—more than you even dreamed of.

You bring Ralph in for an "interview," which basically turns into a love fest. And the siren song gets louder and louder. His resume already had you salivating, but he proceeds to tell you stories about how his team led the acquisitions of companies just like yours. He talks about Jim, who leads the corporate development group at the "big gorilla" company in your space. He regales you with college stories of Jim or how he plays golf with him on the third Tuesday of every month. Ralph is the answer to many a late-night prayer!

Not only does Ralph know the right people, he impresses you with his industry knowledge. His role at that industry titan means he worked with the teams that set the gold standard for the industry. And it means he knows the right people when it comes time to sell your company! Bringing Ralph on board seems like an absolute no-brainer.

You're Not Dell or PepsiCo . . . And That's a Good Thing

Not so fast. There's a key problem here that many entrepreneurs fail to see until it's too late: entrepreneurial, middle-market, high-growth companies are COMPLETELY different animals than Fortune 500 companies. Ralph may have what it takes to run a $500 million department at PepsiCo, but that doesn't mean he's cut out to lead your tiny startup! He may have connections, but it sure is easier to get people to take calls from Ralph at PepsiCo, than Ralph at PissAntCo! That big-company experience got you salivating, but it doesn't necessarily translate.

People who are successful at entrepreneurial companies have one thing in common, regardless of their educational background, employment history, or industry experience: they are all, well, entrepreneurial. They roll up their sleeves, get their hands dirty, and make things happen. They live for this shit. They work long hours because they can't help it—their minds are on, 24/7.

Don't get me wrong; being an executive vice president at a large company is a challenge in so many ways, but it's different than being employee No. 4 at a $1 million company hoping to grow to $10 million ASAP. At the enterprise level, Ralph had resources that are unimaginable for entrepreneurs. He probably had an assistant, ten people who reported to him, project managers, and all the resources he needed to tackle any problem. That just ain't how we roll down here in startup world!

But most entrepreneurs simply can't resist the quick fix that the idea of Resume Ralph brings to the table. And, if I'm being honest, I can't blame them. Every entrepreneur who has been at it for more than a hot minute wants a silver-bullet fix to make their sleepless nights go away.

"Here's What We Did at ______"

When you hire a new leader—any type of leader—we encourage an onboarding period to allow them some runway to get to know the business, the industry, and your team, inside and out. We cover onboarding at length in Intermission IV, beginning on page 215—but what we DON'T want is for the new leader to come in guns blazing, making major changes before they even know where the breakroom is! These expectations should be laid out in the interview process, so you're aligned with each other. We've seen a number of paths that Resume Ralph takes in the first few months that provide hints that he might not be the right long-term fit. Here are a few of the most common:

Jumping to Conclusions

Since Ralph is a seasoned veteran, he might come in HOT! Without getting to know the business, the team, and the lay of the land, he starts changing everything. He already has all the answers. He saw what worked at his Fortune 500 company or whatever hot-shit startup he worked at—saying things like, "Here's what we did at Facebook." Maybe he's thinking, *I don't need to waste time asking questions; I know what we need to do.* He may even want to make big personnel moves before he settles in. All red flags. Look, I'm not saying that shaking things up is necessarily a bad idea, but Ralph needs to get to know the company before he starts going crazy.

Let's assume you made it through the initial onboarding period with Ralph. Even if you haven't noticed cracks forming in the dam yet—if you've hired a true Resume Ralph, the leaks will soon begin to appear.

Big Company Stuff

Fast-forward to the meeting where Ralph starts making suggestions. You're excited to hear what he has to say. You did bring him in because of his industry experience, after all. But you feel like his suggestions completely miss the mark, especially if he comes from a large company with endless resources. Instead of suggesting ways to build out the infrastructure you need to meet increasing demand, he tells you he knows the perfect consultant to do just that. Instead of working on ways to drive sales, he suggests a complete overhaul of the brand by a Madison Avenue advertising agency, along with a million-dollar marketing campaign.

In short, he just doesn't get it. He's not in his comfort zone anymore, where high-dollar ad campaigns are the norm and throwing money at consultants to "figure it out" is commonplace. He's going to have to get his hands dirty, and most Resume Ralphs simply can't or won't do that.

The Kickass PowerPoint

A telltale sign I've seen over the years will seem weird and not exactly scientific, but it's crazy how often it's been true. If Ralph prepares a bells-and-whistles PowerPoint that looks professionally prepared, be careful. It seems to be a big company way to baffle you with bullshit and even mask his deficiencies. Spending tons of time preparing a slick presentation is cool and all, but it takes more than that to build a successful entrepreneurial company. Don't get distracted by how pretty the information is, focus on what Ralph is saying. Does it make sense for a growth-minded startup? Or is this a dog and pony show designed to get you to spend money for someone else to do his job?

This Just Isn't Going to Work

The final straw for a lot of my friends and clients who end up with a Resume Ralph develops over time. As I said above, the "roll up your sleeves and get your hands dirty" mentality is a requirement for growing companies. While I certainly don't advocate for overworking yourself and your team, there is merit to the idea that hard work and long hours are necessary when you're building an entrepreneurial company and taking it to the promised land.

You'd do whatever it takes to make your company successful, and at the end of the day, you need a partner in the foxhole with you. Your mind is working all the time, not because it has to, but because that's who you are! You're always thinking about your product or service and how to drive the company's success!

But Resume Ralph isn't interested in hard work. Maybe he feels that he's already "made it" because of his big-time experience. Maybe he thought working in a "small time" company would be easier than managing a team of 300 people. Or maybe he wanted the perks of being on the ground floor of a rocket ship company, but he didn't realize the level of effort that would be required!

Ultimately, when Ralph leaves the office at 3:00 every day and doesn't check his email after hours, he's not in the right world. Golf dates with muckity-mucks from his former company are great if they lead to relationships for your company. But it sure seems like Ralph uses them as an excuse to take an afternoon off.

At the end of the day, Resume Ralph just isn't the right fit for an entrepreneurial company. He either doesn't get what it takes to succeed, or doesn't want to do what it takes.

Real-World Example

Collin's a friend of mine who founded a consumer-packaged goods (CPG) company that specializes in a snack food found in convenience stores across the country. Collin did a decent job breaking into convenience stores and some grocery stores, including a very well-known national chain. But neither Collin nor his investor group believed he had the experience to grow the company from $1 million in annual revenues to $10 million—much less their ultimate goal of $25 million.

Collin's a product guy. He developed an innovative product and he was good at marketing. But he wasn't a "run the company" kind of guy. And without bringing in someone to help, he was getting burned out and his investors were concerned about whether the company could scale. That's when Collin met his Resume Ralph.

Ralph had twenty years of experience at the major player in his industry who gobbles up successful CPG companies like Collin's. The promise of connections to a future acquirer was attractive for Collin. Equally as important, Ralph left there three years ago and had stints at two other early-stage CPG companies. On paper, he had a perfect blend of big company and entrepreneurial experience.

In their first meeting, Collin was blown away by Ralph, who talked a lot about his experience at the big company, making sure to name-drop all the right people. What really got Collin's attention was that Ralph seemed to understand the types of moves Collin's company needed to make, saying things like, "You need to meet Shawn at 7-Eleven. We get into 7-Eleven, and our credibility and revenue will skyrocket." Collin was smitten.

After hiring Ralph, Collin was able to attract additional investors. While they may not have believed in Collin's ability to scale the company, they loved the potential that Ralph brought to the table with his industry experience and big-time connections. And they loved his PowerPoints in investor presentations. Collin's decision to hire Ralph made him look like a genius—at first.

The first sign for Collin was just a few days in, when Ralph started pushing to hire a buddy of his at a New York advertising agency to overhaul the branding and marketing for the Texas-based company. We're not talking minor tweak or small price tag; we're talking about a several-hundred-thousand-dollar endeavor. While the rebrand may have been needed, there are scrappier ways to do it than giving a blank check to a mega-agency that happens to be run by Ralph's good friend. And this was well before Ralph had an opportunity to get to know the brand or their customers!

The real problem for the company at that time was a production issue at their co-packing facility. They weren't producing in a timely manner, so the company was behind on product deliveries. Ralph took point on solving the issue and immediately hired a consultant friend to get to the bottom of it. After sixty days and LOTS of consulting dollars spent, the suggestion was that they—a relatively tiny $1 million company that was losing money—simply find someone to loan them $5 million to build a brand-new production facility so they could produce their own products in-house. What?

But aside from the fact that Ralph just didn't seem to get it, Collin started recognizing other challenges over the first few months. Specifically, around Ralph's work ethic. He had been a successful executive previously and was more interested in hanging out with his adult kids and his grandkids than he was working hard for Collin's company. He left the office nearly every day at 3:00 to work out and refused to answer his phone or emails until 9:00 the next morning. That's simply not how startups work!

In a less-than-ten-person company, Ralph just wasn't putting in the work necessary to grow the business. Collin called me several times to complain, "Kurt, this dude doesn't work very hard! He's treating this like a lifestyle business." I'll be honest, I really wanted Ralph to be the solution, so I'd calm Collin down with advice like, "He's just getting to know the business, be patient!"

But I was wrong. It turned out that Ralph just wasn't the right fit. And the longer he stayed, the deeper the hole Collin had to dig out of. So, Collin made the scary-but-right move to let Ralph go. He then put on his big-boy pants and faced his investors and board to explain the situation, along with his plan to replace Ralph with the right operating partner to scale the company.

Do You Think You Have a Resume Ralph?

First and foremost, let's pause for a second to say that the resume isn't the only thing that matters here. There are many great, hardworking, capable minds who work at large companies. While the transition from Fortune 500 to startup isn't easy, it's one that some have indeed successfully made. So don't automatically think you have a Resume Ralph just because he has a brand name on his bio.

But if you think you have a Ralph, cruise over to Intermission II for some tips on what to do, as well as some ideas on how to keep Ralph out of your company in the first place. I've seen a number of these guys and gals in my career, including my own businesses and several I've invested in! Anybody can make this mistake, but we want to reduce your risk—or at least minimize the damage.

YES
NO
MAYBE

08

PIPELINE PAUL

THE SILVER BULLET SALES GUY

"The transition from heroic founder-led sales to professionalized sales is massive. Entrepreneurs often look for the silver bullet by hiring a senior leader with a track record running large sales teams. However, leading a mature team is a far cry from ***being*** *the team. They often fail because they don't share the founder's passion and they don't have what it takes to sell in a startup environment."*

– **Rand Stagen,** CEO of Stagen Leadership Academy

For many early-stage companies, the entrepreneur IS the sales engine. The business has grown as a result of the founder's expansive network and reputation. Sure, the operations team does great work that builds relationships and creates satisfied clients, but the initial sale is often related to one (or maybe two) rainmakers.

But relying on the heroic efforts of a few makes next-level growth impossible. Many companies can't cross the chasm from "scrappy startup" to "scale." The suggested solutions often range from "we need a junior [insert rainmaker's name here]" to "let's hire a bunch of hungry and aggressive salespeople, throw 'em together, and see who survives!"

There are many potential paths for founders to consider when looking to drive sales. But Rockstar salespeople who end up working out are hard to find and even harder to hire. I've seen so many entrepreneurs struggle hiring salespeople. Partially because most salespeople (even the bad ones) are pretty darn good at selling themselves in the interview process! Unfortunately, those skills don't always translate to selling your product or service.

One common way we've seen this play out is when you end up with a salesperson who talks a good game and is very positive about their sales pipeline—one that always seems to be in the future. They seem to have something BIG just around the corner. But for some reason or another, it rarely pans out. You start thinking that even THEY don't believe those opportunities will ever come to fruition! But what the hell do you do? At that point, unfortunately, your eggs are truly only in one basket!

If any of this resonates, read on. This particular chapter will focus on "Paul" in a sales role and what to do about him, not necessarily as a sales leader.

The Problem for the Entrepreneur

There are a number of paths that can lead to Pipeline Paul clogging up your business with unfulfilled promises and a "tomorrow" that never seems to come. In my experience, Paul often comes "highly recommended" by a trusted source. Maybe Paul is a friend of a friend, or even someone you feel pressured to please (like an investor).

More on that later. Before we get to Paul though, let's talk about what's happening behind the scenes in companies that end up turning to him for answers.

As an entrepreneur, you spent the early days wearing every hat imaginable. Hell, you probably developed the product, led the team, drove sales, and even vacuumed the office floors! You sold AND delivered—people saw you as the brand. Everything went through you.

As a startup, you can thrive on the herculean efforts of a few. But as you grow and evolve, you need more revenue to feed the beast. You realize that the business needs to grow beyond a single rainmaker for it to continue to thrive. I've seen a number of methods used to solve this challenge, and some of them even work!

I once moved one of my key lieutenants over to sales in an effort to take some of the load off of me. She did fairly well, considering the circumstances. One team member told another employee that as long as he was fed a steady diet of referrals and connections from me and my network, he was great! In fact, he jokingly referred to these leads coming from the "revenue fairy," and he'd sit idly by waiting for them to show up. But the revenue fairy can't save you forever. If you want to scale your business, you have to move beyond the rainmaker's network.

You're forward-thinking, so you see this as an opportunity to move up-market and sell to bigger companies: enterprises with household-name logos you can show off on your website—companies that can write big checks! To do this, you must professionalize your organization, and it starts with your sales process and sales team. Even if you don't have a sales team in the classical sense, everyone has, or needs, a sales process.

To get to the next level, you'll need investments in systems, processes, and infrastructure. You'll need to develop a compensation structure that aligns the sales team's incentives with the company's goals and the culture you've instilled. In short, you need to do things differently. The approach that got you here definitely won't get you where you want to go!

The Silver Bullet: Most entrepreneurs don't think about investments in systems, processes, and infrastructure—they usually go right to bringing in the silver bullet hire to solve everything, especially in sales. Check out Intermission I for some best hiring practices.

Everyone Has a "Perfect" Candidate

Once you've determined it's time to find that Rockstar, you do what you've always done. You start talking to people you trust. You tell your friends, peers, and business partners that you're looking to upgrade sales—and free advice flows! First, your YPO or Vistage group advises you to hire a sales leader and your executive coach encourages you to "work ON your business, not IN your business." Someone even gives you a job description they used for their VP of sales search last year.

And once you've decided to start looking for a new

salesperson, something weird happens. Everyone and their dog has candidates for you. Your banker, your lawyer, and your benefits broker walk into a bar—wait, no, this isn't a joke. They all tell you they know "a guy who is perfect for you!" Seems like every sales guy who is "in transition" (or out of work) is referred to you!

You try to listen and nod along to all of these "perfect" fits, but candidly, it's become very noisy. Then someone you really respect tells you about Pipeline Paul—and she's adamant that Paul is your guy. You meet Paul and boy, are you impressed. You fall in love with him and shortly thereafter, he's your new VP of Sales! Thus begins the story of Pipeline Paul.

Who is Pipeline Paul?

Paul is a sales guy. He seems to be a damn good one. Everyone seems to like him. If you ask his neighbors, they'll say he's fun to be around, he has a million-dollar smile, and he's great at parties. He brings a good bottle of wine and becomes friends with all the important people by the end of the night. He looks you in the eyes when he shakes your hand, and he remembers your name.

Paul sounds great on the surface; that's why you fell in love with him! But now that you've gotten to know him, work with him, and dig deeper into who he is, things start falling apart. You find out he's "all hat and no cattle," as we say in Texas—all show and no substance. He talks a big game. He's always JUST ABOUT to close the next million-dollar deal, "just waiting on final approval." He's built an impressive pipeline of enterprise-level deals. He tells you about potential deals with your dream companies—feeding right into your desire to put some high-profile pelts on the wall.

But as great as those deals sound, they stay in the pipeline. He tells you they "should close next week," then "next week" . . . and then "next week." Paul just keeps pushing the dates back, saying things like, "These are complicated deals!" or "This is the big leagues, these aren't mom-and-pop deals anymore." or "Be patient, everything will be fine." He keeps promising BIG results soon.

But "soon" never seems to come. With Paul, it's always in the pipeline. And no matter how much you want to believe (and, oh boy, do you want to believe!), no matter how much time, leeway, and resources you give him, it never seems to work out.

Hope Is Not a Strategy

If you find yourself constantly waiting for deals in the pipeline to close—and days turn into weeks, which stretch into months—you have a serious problem on your hands. It's not just that Pipeline Paul isn't doing his job, he's preventing your business from moving forward. You're not really sure whether the deals Paul's promising will come through. As a result, you simply can't plan for the future when you can't trust your sales projections.

This is where it gets really hard. You WANT to believe that Paul will come through, but you fear he's full of crap. You've invested so much time, energy, and hope in Paul, praying he'll come through. Not to mention the money you've invested; probably hundreds of thousands of dollars in salary and benefits at this point. But what hurts the most is the time—time you'll never get back.

For entrepreneurial companies, time is a precious commodity. And Paul always seems to need more of it. But with every Pipeline Paul, the clock eventually strikes midnight. You've seen enough, and you decide something has to be done.

Real-World Example

Kyle's a close friend, founder and CEO of Zivea, a healthcare software company. In just a few years, his team developed a stellar product and had acquired a number of name-recognizable healthcare clients off the back of Kyle's personal brand and network. The company's reputation grew.

Zivea evolved from a scrappy startup to a "real" company looking to scale and grow from $5 to $20 million in annual sales. Zivea had the perfect combination of great product, fantastic service, and solid reputation. Once one hospital in a system adopted the software, other hospital administrators in the system followed suit. In a relatively short period of time, Zivea's software was being used in three of the top ten healthcare systems in the country. Excited to take his company to the next level, Kyle began to think about seizing the opportunity by professionalizing his sales team with Rockstar talent.

As usual, when a founder starts looking for top talent, Kyle's network became an echo chamber of "you gotta meet this guy!" and "she's the best salesperson I've ever worked with!" In short order, "perfect" candidates were coming at him from all angles.

Enter Pipeline Paul. His background was stellar. He worked at three of America's largest healthcare companies, so he had relationships with many of the people Kyle wanted to sell to. In retrospect, there was one red flag on Paul's resume: his tenure at each of his last three employers was just under two years. In Kyle's defense, it's easy to overlook some details when you fall in love with the idea of that silver bullet.

And Paul was impressive! Dare I say it—he was a STUD. He said all the right things, name-dropped the right people, and talked extensively about the relationships he had with numerous other top companies. Hell, he played golf last week with a key executive at Zivea's top target! If there was a playbook for how to impress in an interview, Paul would've written it. Oh, and he had plausible answers for leaving at the two-year mark for his last three roles (one company was sold, the next one was "borderline unethical," and the last one "simply couldn't deliver on what I was selling!").

Kyle quickly hired Paul, excited to cash in on his relationships. During his first thirty days, things seemed on track. Paul spent time getting to know the product, the company, and existing client relationships. But Kyle's an entrepreneur who spends more time doing than thinking—and he wanted Paul doing more doing. In weekly meetings, Kyle encouraged Paul to reach out to his contacts, but Paul had excuses at the ready. Saying things like, "I don't want to until we have first-class marketing collateral, this stuff isn't professional. We need to make a great first impression." Kyle didn't understand. He wanted Paul to just DO it, not sit around waiting for perfection!

Finally, Paul did start setting up meetings with his big-company contacts. A weekend of golf here, a fancy dinner there, and even a trip to the US Open—but nothing resulted in the big deals Paul promised. In the weekly meetings, he seemed to be getting more defensive: "These big deals take time. I'm working on a whale, dammit." He sure did sound impressive, but Kyle wanted results. And that expense account—holy smokes!

One year in, and Kyle was growing more and more frustrated. But Paul had a huge opportunity that looked very promising (and intoxicating!). In sixty days, he would present Zivea's software solution to the leadership team of a very large hospital system: one deal would make everything worthwhile! Kyle was cautiously optimistic. Over the next few months, the meeting got pushed back, then canceled, then rescheduled with a sub-segment of the leadership team. Kyle was losing his mind!

Eighteen months into Paul's tenure, Kyle was beginning to see why Paul left each of those companies after two years: it didn't appear that he could close. And once that became clear, his very large expense account and huge salary weighed very heavily on the books.

Around that time, the economy shifted, and Kyle's hand was forced. He had to cut costs and letting Paul go was an obvious choice. Paul still had big deals in the pipeline even as he left, but Kyle had ZERO confidence that he would have been able to bag any of the elephants he was hunting.

After letting Paul go, Kyle was surprised when another member of the sales team approached him—someone who reported directly to Paul. "What took you so long?" he asked. Other team members made similar comments. "Remember that presentation he gave a couple months ago? I was actually the one who put it all together!" This is actually very common; the entrepreneur is the last to know!

Keeping Paul Out of Your Pipeline

Want some tips on how to keep Paul out of your pipeline or what to do once you realize you're saddled with a Pipeline Paul? Check out Intermission II for tips, tidbits, and things to think about. Lord knows I've seen a ton of these guys in my career—either with clients or my own damn business! No one is immune, but hopefully we can help you dodge a bullet or fix the problem quickly.

INTERMISSION II

EXECUTIVE-LEVEL HIRES

"Great vision without great people is irrelevant."

— **Jim Collins** in *Good to Great*[5]

Not surprisingly, as co-founder of one of the top executive search firms in Texas, I get asked a million questions about how to recruit great employees. Questions like: "Where do I find them?" "How can I convince them to work for me?" and "How much do I pay them?"

But I'm also asked—pretty much daily—what to do about underperforming "leaders," how to deal with pain-in-the-ass partners, and how to get rid of employees who simply aren't cut out for entrepreneurial companies. What people DON'T ask me, at least not often enough, is how to AVOID these future problems in the first place. I'd like to help you reduce the risk that you end up with one of these clowns on your team.

In the last three chapters, I introduced three common executive hires I've seen affect high-growth companies. If you want to avoid hiring Resume Ralph, figure out how to repurpose Techno Tim, or fire Pipeline Paul, this chapter is for you! In the following pages, I'll offer some advice, answer common questions and concerns, and outline courses of action so you have a few ideas of what to do when you're faced with any or all of these characters.

Before we dive in though, a quick reminder: There's no silver bullet. There's no one-size-fits-all solution to these problems. Every scenario, every personality, and every relationship is different. We're dealing with human beings, after all! I definitely don't have all the answers, but I've seen these situations many times with my own teams and a ton of clients. Think of this chapter as a workbook of lessons learned the hard way!

Create a Culture of Accountability

The absolute BEST thing you can do as an entrepreneur is to establish a culture of accountability on your team. This will help you in every aspect of your business, not just mitigating the risk of bad employees.

I'm an entrepreneur, I'm not good at holding people accountable . . .

Yep—and that's why this one is hard for me personally. I absolutely SUCK at holding people accountable and I firmly believe most entrepreneurs share this trait. I'm a great leader when I have a team of go-getters and self-starters who hold THEMSELVES accountable. But as the team gets bigger, that self-managed style doesn't work if we haven't established an accountability culture.

As such, I've learned to partner with strong operators like Brett Lawson at The Controller Group and Cisco Sacasa at HireBetter to align goals, set expectations, and hold my team accountable. This allows me to focus on what I do best and leverage everyone's strengths and skills.

But Kurt, I don't have a Brett or a Cisco!

If you are an entrepreneur (or work with one) who doesn't have an operating partner yet, I highly recommend skipping ahead to chapters 11 and 12, RIGHT NOW, to begin exploring that concept. In the meantime, you may want to bring in an advisor, consultant, or friend who is a strong operator to help you. Ideally, they can help you create the systems and processes necessary to know when things are going off the rails BEFORE the train runs off the track. The earlier you take these steps, the better.

What does this mean?

One example of a "system and process" that will help drive accountability is leveraging a customer relationship management, or CRM tool for your sales team. A good CRM, used properly, can track and report everything relevant to managing them—calls, meetings, proposals, expenses . . . you get the picture. You'll obviously want to track revenue, but that is a lagging indicator. In my experience, if the sales team is competent and putting in the work, revenue will follow.

The CRM will give you the ability to track your team's efforts—leading indicators—independent of revenue. You build accountability around the data generated by the system, and it's no longer easy for a bad employee (like Pipeline Paul) to hide. Instituting a culture of accountability is one of the best ways to mitigate getting caught up in his web of lies and deceit.

But I still need help . . . now!

I realize that most of what I recommend is more strategic, bigger picture—for the long haul. But I get it; you need help now. I just don't want you to panic and make a bad hire, which will make your situation ten times worse. So, let's look at how we can AVOID making a bad hire, but more importantly, how you can make a GREAT hire.

How to Keep Paul (and Ralph and Tim) Out of Your Pipeline

First line of defense? Don't hire them in the first place. Sounds easy, right? I've seen a bunch of these guys in my career. Some I've even hired myself! In fact, I recently had one whose strategy appeared to be telling me repeatedly how awesome I was as a leader. I love compliments—but damn, spend less time kissing my ass and more time closing deals! Although I've seen my share of these guys, I've also dodged some bullets and picked up some tricks along the way.

So, how the hell do I avoid these guys?

Until you have an operating partner (or Integrator), consider identifying someone you trust from outside the organization to serve as your advisor or consultant during the interview process—especially for executive-level hires. I chose someone who knows me and my organization well: someone I trusted to be a great interviewer and had the company's best interest at heart. In my case I asked Mike Aviles, one of my YPO forum mates, to help. But I've seen clients and friends ask their Vistage chairs, EOS Implementers, members of their board, or friends, among others.

It's important to have this independent perspective. I've seen many entrepreneurs make the mistake of asking their employees to interview executive-level hires. But it's very hard for legacy employees to be unbiased when interviewing someone who will professionalize the organization (i.e., "change the way we've always done it"). This is especially true for employees who will report to the new executive. There's a natural inclination to want to protect the status quo; in some cases, the legacy employee wants to protect their fiefdom or their direct line to you. Consider involving them from a cultural perspective by having them meet your final candidate(s) for a get-to-know-you dinner, but don't have them grill the finalist(s) for hours in the conference room.

I'm not immune to this advice. Even though I co-founded a recruiting firm, I personally suck at hiring. Ironic, right? But as the optimistic, glass-half-full kind of guy, I usually see the best in people. If I interview three COO candidates, I'll probably want to hire and create roles for all of them!

But good operators? They stay focused, ask sharp questions, and aren't trying to make buddies out of these candidates. They're not as close to the business as you are, so they're less likely to make hiring decisions based on emotions. They'll make sure the person on the other side of the table has the capacity and ability to be my next-level COO. In short, they're great interviewing partners for me—and I'm betting they'll be good for you too.

In the meantime . . .

OK, OK, but I think I found "the one." I mean, look at this resume!

Their resume might be awesome, but be careful. This ain't their first rodeo. They know all the buzzwords to get you salivating about their background. On the surface, they've worked for very successful companies and had impressive titles. You're starstruck. How's this guy even available?! But look closer. You may notice a few things. For example, are most of his recent stints very short—like less than two years at each of them?

Less than two years? What does that mean?

Usually, it means each of his previous employers gave him about a year's worth of leash before they stopped buying his bullshit and let him go. This was especially true for Pipeline Paul, because in sales, it typically takes six to twelve months to get rolling. Then he buys himself another six months with his "it's in the pipeline" rhetoric.

Another reason to dig deeper is because this area is ripe for gamesmanship. I've seen many resumes that simply show the YEARS employed, with no mention of the MONTHS. This can be misleading, especially when we're talking about two years. For example, a tenure of "2017 to 2019" on a resume, may actually be November

1, 2017 to January 31, 2019—just fourteen months. Trust me, I've seen it!

But he's got plausible answers for why he left each gig.

Maybe he claims his previous boss was an ethical nightmare. Or operations wasn't equipped to handle some supply chain issues. Or management was too risk averse. The reason is irrelevant to him, as long as you buy it. And of course, he has answers for each of your concerns! Most executive candidates will rehearse—and even be coached—especially for the tough questions.

The key here is you've got to keep digging. Did Ralph truly "leave" his previous position or was he about to get the boot? Was Tim truly at odds with a risk averse CEO who couldn't get out of his own way? If you dig a little, you may find that the CEO was simply tired of Tim's ego and was days away from letting him go!

He worked for a highly reputable Fortune 500 company. They must have seen something in him, right?

One of the bigger mistakes I see entrepreneurs make comes with candidates from big companies, household names. Just because they had a successful career at a large company you respect doesn't mean their skills will translate to your startup. Think about it: your revenue is $10 million annually, and their last gig was a $10 billion (with a B!) corporation. Many of the traits you need at your stage—grit, problem-solving, curiosity, and a roll-up-your-sleeves mentality—are NOT typically traits that make someone successful in a billion-dollar multinational.

More often than not, you'll see these candidates struggle when they don't have access to the people, resources, and brand name their previous employer provided.

OK, got it. Big company is a no-go.

Not necessarily. As I mentioned, this isn't one-size-fits-all, and it's not only about the resume. Just don't fall for the siren song when you see that name brand company experience. Be aware of the differences between your company and their previous employer so you can ask the right questions. There are loads of great, hardworking, and capable minds at enterprise-level companies who desire something more meaningful and impactful. The transition isn't easy, but it can be done.

How can I tell which big-company experience will translate?

Don't just look at the name of the company—ask thoughtful questions. What did they do there? For example, if they started the Latin American division at Disney with two employees and $1 million in revenue and grew that division to a hundred employees and $100 million in revenue, they likely have some entrepreneurial spirit and a get-shit-done mentality! If they launched a new and innovative product at P&G, those skills will likely translate to your startup. But if they managed a $1 billion brand at PepsiCo with a $50 million marketing budget, they may not be the right chief marketing officer for your $5 million snack food company.

Ask probing questions about their experience and the resources, assistance, and oversight provided by their previous employer to get a better idea for how their talents might translate.

I don't get it; his bosses all had good things to say.

While you're conducting due diligence into a candidate's employment history, make sure you also reach out to people who worked alongside him. Bosses often don't see everything, or they are unwilling to admit their failures. When you ask the right questions, you may find that someone else was propping Paul up. He was the sales leader, so of course he looked great (and took credit) when the team was successful! But in reality, his subordinate was the reason for that success. Without doing your due diligence, you might end up with Pipeline Paul when you could have had Closer Carl!

I got all that, but this guy comes highly recommended by someone I trust!

Beware of the "opportunistic" hire. When your network finds out you're looking for a new sales leader, CFO, or even head janitor, you'll get bombarded with loads of "perfect" candidates. You feel obligated to listen because the lead came from your board, a key investor, or friend you trust. More often than not, these "perfect" candidates just happen to be in career transition.

Think about this: Why is it that you never seem to receive "perfect fit" referrals when the candidate is gainfully employed? Why are they always "in transition"? I'm not saying bad things can't happen to good people, but every single time? Think about that the next time someone sends you their cousin, their wife's friend's husband, or the coach of their kid's soccer team.

Do you have any interview tips?

I've got a bunch, but here are my two favorites. The first is based on what I often tell people are the most important factors in team-building—trust, respect, and communication. You've got to start laying the foundation DURING THE INTERVIEW PROCESS! Especially for these senior-level hires. Get to know your finalists and establish a rapport. Communicate exactly what you're looking for and expecting from them should they be hired for the position. Set the stage for open communication, even before you bring them on board. Go beyond pleasantries and make sure they have what it takes for your entrepreneurial role.

The second is one of my personal go-tos, but it takes work. As you get down to two or three finalists, present them with an actual problem you're facing. Allow them to meet the team so they can assess the situation and understand the resources available to tackle the problem. Ask them to present how they would proceed. You get to see how they think and operate—and you get some free advice. From Resume Ralph, if Collin had asked Ralph how he'd address the production problem, he might have avoided countless future headaches. If your candidate can't or won't develop a reasonable response, they aren't the right fit or aren't serious about your opportunity!

I'm smitten by this one. She's exactly what we need!

I implore you to avoid getting drawn in by the silver bullet. I like to say that I fall in love with "the concept" of Ralph and ask my team to keep me honest. Tune out the noise of name-dropping and storytelling to get to the soft skills you're looking for—a willingness to roll up their sleeves and get stuff done, not sit in an ivory tower and point. They've got to have grit, drive to be successful, and willingness to do what it takes to get there. Brand names mean nothing if you don't have grit.

Ugh. I don't know if I'm cut out for hiring!

You and me both! As I said, I suck at hiring—mainly because I'm an optimist and find the positives in everyone! But the key is I KNOW THAT. That's why my job in the interview process isn't to screen and vet candidates; it's to sell the vision and help determine culture fit.

In my case, I tell my team not to let anyone get through to me if they're not 1,000 percent confident they can do the job. And as I mentioned earlier, for senior-level positions, I bring in someone from the outside to serve as my operating partner, an advisor to assist me in the interview process.

You've got this. Just play to your strengths and leverage those around you, as needed.

What if I've got one on my team?

Sometimes we simply make mistakes, no matter how hard we try! And that's OK. When you realize you've made a bad hire, whether you fell for a seemingly killer resume, the unfulfilled promises of amazing connections, or the smartest-person-in-the-room tech wizard, don't worry, you're not alone! You're also not alone when you realize there's a member (or members) of your team you've outgrown or who simply aren't cutting it in their current role.

When you realize you've made a mistake or have employees who aren't getting it done, you usually have three options: (1) coach them into the leader you need them to be; (2) move them to a different role; or (3) terminate their employment.

We cover those three options and how best to choose which one is right for you in Intermission I, beginning on page 81.

09

B-PLAYER BOB

ROLE PLAYERS ARE PEOPLE TOO

"Sure, we've had our share of superstars over the years but it's the role players who made the great teams great. The guys who showed up to work every day, worked hard, knew their role, and did their job with no drama—those are the guys who put us over the top."

– **Dave Van Horn,** Arkansas Razorbacks Head Baseball Coach and SEC Coach of the Year 2021

Every year, the NBA awards a "Sixth Man of the Year" to the best player in the league who isn't a starter on their team but comes off the bench and helps them win. Some people might find this award a little silly. You're telling a professional athlete he's the best player on the bench; he's not good enough to be in the starting lineup. It's kind of a strange concept, but in fairness, it's helpful when a player knows his role on the team and doesn't need to be the star. He's a B-player.

While the NBA Sixth Man is not the best player on his team, he produces when he gets his chance. Sometimes he wows you with his play, but mostly it's just solid and dependable. He might get you up out of your seat with a huge dunk, draw a critical foul, or—every now and then—hit a big shot, but his best attribute is his dependability.

Not a basketball fan? Let's try football. The 2020 Kansas City Chiefs backup QB was Chad Henne. He wasn't going to threaten All-Pro Patrick Mahomes for his starting job, nor was he expected to lead them to the Super Bowl. But he was a great practice player, a good teammate, and a solid backup. When Mahomes went down with a concussion toward the end of a close playoff game in January 2021, Chiefs fans were sweating. It was B-player Henne who came off the bench and picked up the first down to ice the game and send the Chiefs to the Super Bowl.

B-Players

The NBA "Sixth Man" and NFL backup QBs are great analogies to folks in the business world known as B-players. They certainly have their place on their teams, and some are even kickass enough to earn a sweet award at the end of the season. But this isn't a book about professional athletes, it's about entrepreneurs!

If you're an entrepreneur, you've probably heard some version of the following statement a thousand times: "You need to hire A-players—the best of the best!" Whether it's a buddy in your CEO networking group, a competitor's LinkedIn page, or your own board of directors, people seem to think that A-player talent is the only way to build your business.

Here's the thing, though—yes, you need superstar level talent like the 1995–96 Chicago Bulls had in Michael Jordan and Scottie Pippen. But you also need talented role players like Bill Wennington, Jud Buechler, and (1996 Sixth Man of the Year) Toni Kukoc. There's a reason those Bulls are considered the best basketball team of all time. Sure, they had A-players leading the way, but they had a competent cast of B-players who, when they played well together, were magical.

Most business books will lie and tell you that you need Rockstars in every role if you want to be successful. But the truth is, B-players are vital parts of your team as well. As long as they're given the right opportunities, put in the right role, and held accountable, they can help you achieve your goals. Chances are you won't be able to scale without B-players on the team.

So What's a B-Player?

Before we go any further, we need to define a few things. There are a number of systems out there to rate talent; with A, B, and C being the most common. One of the more well-known versions is from Brad Smart in his book *Topgrading*.[6] He defines A-players as "high performers, the top 10 percent of talent," while B-players are "disappointing, the next 25 percent," and C-players are "mediocre performers, the bottom 65 percent." Candidly, I'm not a big fan of B-players being rated as "disappointing." (More on that later.)

Smart goes on to say the best way to determine if the candidate you're interviewing is an A-player is to simply ask him or her, "How would your previous bosses rate your performance on a scale of excellent, very good, good, fair, and poor?" This actually seems like an odd method, since most of the A-players I know—ones I'd want on my team—are humble and don't brag on themselves!

But that's not my only problem with *Topgrading* and many of the other books on the subject. Many of the so-called hiring gurus will tell you that you should ONLY hire A-players. Honestly, that sounds like a great goal. And if you have unlimited cash, your company's a unicorn, and you've got the sex appeal of Tesla or Google, maybe you can commit to hiring only A-level talent. Did I mention unlimited cash?

But in the real world, entrepreneurial teams are a mix of legacy employees who have been with you awhile, solid players who are good for where you are now, and A-players who will take you to the next level. Some of the non–A-players have great potential, but others are just hard-working people who are steady producers and are willing to do what it takes to help the company be successful.

Sure, there will almost always be some employees you need to transition out and upgrade their positions. But for most of us, there's no magical moment where you simply clean house by firing all your problematic legacy employees and shore up your org chart with nothing but A-players. So let me state for the record that IF you find yourself in a situation where you can hire all "A-players" as defined by *Topgrading*—be my guest! But if you're in the real world like the rest of us scrappy entrepreneurs out here, then the rest of this chapter is for you.

My Definitions

To me, an A-player is someone who thrives in their current role and always pushes the envelope, developing new skills to help the company grow. They take responsibilities and challenges head-on. They're leaders and mentors who put the company first. You want as many A-players on your team as possible, then get the hell out of their way! Here are some additional bullet points for A-players:

- High-Performer
- Self-Motivated
- Gritty
- Competitive
- Problem-Solver
- Curious
- Passionate
- Committed
- Charismatic with an ability to energize
- Wants to work with other A-players

Synonyms for A-players include Rockstar, game-changer, superstar, all-star, and high performer, among others—and I use these terms interchangeably.

A B-player is someone who's usually competent at doing their current job, but is failing to take the next step—for now. They MAY have the ability to grow into an A-player with the right opportunities and guidance. They aren't visionary or highly driven but are vital to entrepreneurial companies because they make up the majority of your employees. They shouldn't be your leaders, as they're best served as individual contributors. Nor should they be hiring new employees because they usually hire C-players! Here are a few B-player bullet points:

- Accurate
- Reliable
- Consistent
- Often need guidance
- Don't often work after hours
- Don't need a ton of oversight
- Rarely go above and beyond
- Won't hire A-players

A C-player is someone who's usually not competent in their current role and definitely isn't able to grow into an A-player. They're generally non-producers. Procrastination is a common trait and they fail to deliver on promises. In short, they're not fit for entrepreneurial companies. I encourage you not to waste time trying to coax C-players along or develop them. Most managers think they're great coaches and can save people, but the reality is this is consistently false. Don't move them around trying to find a home. You'll be wasting your time and theirs—and you may lose some much-needed A- or B-players by focusing too much time on non-performers. A few C-player characteristics:

- Pessimistic
- Dramatic
- Unreliable
- Bring down morale
- Frequently make mistakes
- Lazy (at least at work)
- Never go above and beyond
- Ignore your requests

Every Team Has B-Players

There's a lot we could talk about with those definitions, but we're going to focus on B-players in this chapter. First and foremost, EVERY TEAM HAS B-PLAYERS. My team at HireBetter, the 1995–96 Bulls, and your team at [insert company name here] all share this inescapable fact. Anyone who tells you they only hire A-players is either full of crap, woefully confused, or just doesn't recognize the role B-players play in entrepreneurial companies.

The keys to managing B-players are understanding that they're on your team and knowing how best to leverage their skill set. As for what to do with them . . . well, as usual, there's no one-size-fits-all approach.

First and foremost, your B-player may be perfectly content in their role as an individual contributor, and they have no hopes or expectations for a larger role. I think that's got to be OK. Not everyone is obsessed with career growth or is wired to go above and beyond to grow the company. Let's appreciate them for who they are and let them do their best work, without us getting in the way.

What about the other ones? The B-players who want to progress their careers?

If your B-player is "failing to take the next step—for now," that means there's hope, right? Maybe it's a lack of knowledge and expertise that's holding them back. Sometimes it's raw talent that hasn't been honed. Or maybe they just haven't exhibited the leadership qualities you're looking for. These issues can usually be addressed with the right leader at the helm.

Diving deeper into next steps, let's consider the personalities at play. Is he or she willing to learn, grow, and develop into an A-player over time? Are they willing to accept a secondary role for now and accept mentorship from someone else? Not everyone is willing to take a backseat—especially if they're a legacy employee used to calling the shots.

Next, consider their potential for growth. Unfortunately, not all B-players have what it takes to be an A-player. And, as we said before, some are content with where they are, which is OK. If they don't have the capacity to develop into an A-player with your company, don't try to shoehorn them in. That's hard for entrepreneurs like me; I like to see the best in everyone. But not everyone has "it."

Finally, how does this person fit your organization as it stands now? If they're not a culture fit, it may be time to exit them, regardless of their capabilities. How are they doing in their current role? Some employees crave growth and power but aren't even handling their current roles well. On the other hand, if they're a strong cultural fit, doing well in their current roles, and consistently taking on more and more responsibilities, they're a candidate for growth.

Ask yourself these questions, adapted from Intermission I: (1) If your B-player quit tomorrow, how would you feel?; and (2) How would you feel if you had ten of them on your team? If the answers to those questions are positive, you might have a future A-player on your hands!

But enough with the hypotheticals. By now, you know that I believe the best way to understand B-players and what to do with them is to share some stories about characters you may come across in your own entrepreneurial journey. Let's get to know Bob.

Introducing B-Player Bob

Bob has been with you for a long time and has always done everything you asked of him. He's become a trusted advisor to you and feels like he can give you open and honest feedback. Because of that, you've developed a mutual trust and respect for each other.

Bob was always OK at his day job, but not overly impressive. He didn't do everything he SHOULD do; he did everything you asked him to do. As the company grew and you hired more people, Bob was being pushed farther and farther away from you. This was tough for him, because he always had a direct line of communication to the big boss.

But as we've seen with Right-Hand Rita, Bounce-Around Betty, and Who's Your Mike, your company simply outgrew members of your team. It happened with B-Player Bob as well. In the past, every time you tried to increase his role and responsibilities, you were disappointed. So he's back to his individual contributor role, which he's doing well in. As much as he wants to grow in stature and title, right now, he's a B-player, and a damn good one at that.

In many cases, founders promote Bob, either because they fear losing him or because they're loyal to him. He's been a trusted confidant, after all. It's only human for you to reward his loyalty with a promotion. But if you were to do that, not only would you be setting both of you up for failure, you'd also likely see one of the most common B-players-as-leaders scenarios play out (which isn't a good thing).

You see, when B-players are leaders and they're in charge of hiring, they hire people who don't threaten their standing in the organization. It's probably not a conscious decision, but it happens time and time again. Bob won't want to hire anyone who could take his job in the future. Instead, he'll hire a team of C-players who make him feel comfortable (and smart). But with a team of C-players, your company is in trouble—and Bob will come up with all kinds of excuses about his team's inability to perform!

When dealing with the B-Player Bobs of the world, make sure you aren't promoting too far, too fast. Perhaps if Bob had demonstrated leadership qualities, you could have engaged an interim leader or a coach to mentor him. But promoting him and hoping he turns into a leader NEVER works. Everybody knows hope isn't a strategy.

Still think the 1995–96 Bulls, arguably the best NBA team of all time, had only A-players? Even by Brad Smart's definition, they weren't all A-players. His definition included "someone whose boss rates their performance excellent or very good, NOT just good."

I'm sorry, but I'm struggling to believe Dennis Rodman's former coach rated him "excellent," since he was labeled a malcontent as he left the San Antonio Spurs. I'm also struggling to believe that Toni Kukoc, Bill Wennington, and Jud Buechler were rated as "very good" by their previous coaches. The bottom line is that the Bulls had Michael Jordan, Scottie Pippen, and a bunch of role players who did the little things to complement those two superstars. B-players were vitally important to the success of that championship team.

Another B-Player: Not-My-Job Barbara

You know I'm a "glass half full" guy who sees potential in people they might not see in themselves. That's how I feel about Barbara, who has a lot in common with Bob. She's been with the company less than a year, but she's very smart and seems to have a strategic mind. In planning sessions, she's quick with ideas and has a good feel for the company's needs. On the surface, she's performing as a B-player with A-player potential.

But man, when you look closer, she sure seems to find ways to shirk responsibilities—even those that are part of her job description. In those same meetings where she's spouting off about the big picture, she somehow escapes with no action items. She's either "too busy to take that on right now" or talks other team members into doing the job. "Bob would be GREAT for this!" she proclaims. Barbara doesn't seem to care who's working nights and weekends, as long as it's not her.

I've had a couple of Barbaras on my teams over the years. Honestly, it's tough for leaders like me to cut through the noise and see the problems Barbara causes. She shows flashes of A-player status at times, but she reverts to C-player status due to her ability to avoid work. If you dig deeper, you'll realize that not only is she actually a C-player—she's a troublemaker and needs to be gone, ASAP.

The worst mistake you could make with Barbara would be to promote her based on her strategic mind and potential. Your culture would take a huge hit and you'd probably lose your A-players and some of your legit B-players as a result.

And Another: Bobby the Rising Star

Bobby's been a solid member of your team the past few years. He does everything you ask of him, he's dependable, and he busts his ass. He's a solid B-player but definitely brings A-player qualities to the table, as well. For example, he's starting to take on more responsibilities and display a strategic mindset around new product development your company needs so desperately.

As you prepare to launch your new product, Bobby's team of one needs to become a team of ten with a strong leader at the helm. You recognize your need for been-there-done-that experience to lead the team. Bobby wants to step into that role, but he doesn't have experience leading or managing people or launching new products. You know he has potential, but you can't throw him to the wolves. This is too important for the company, and it wouldn't be fair to him. So you decide to pair him with an experienced leader (either as a full-time employee or a part-time consultant) and let him learn under their tutelage.

As we discussed in previous chapters, it's time to have tough, but important, conversations with him about the company's future—and his role in it. You know you need someone experienced to lead the team, but you don't want to risk losing Bobby, the rising star. This is a hard conversation, but I like to frame it as an opportunity for him and his career. If he's able to learn and be mentored, you see him as a future leader for your organization (or even someone else's down the road).

Bobby can take this conversation in a number of ways. He might accept the opportunity and take it in stride, doubling down on the A-player qualities you recognize in him. And in a year or so, you might see that he's ready to take on the leadership role himself.

On the other hand, he might react negatively to being told he's not ready. "If I'm a rising star, why not give me the opportunity?" he may ask. That's a fair question in many situations, but you have to decide what's best for the company. Especially if you're a first-time entrepreneur, it's important you surround yourself with people who have previous experience in similar situations. If Bobby doesn't have the emotional maturity to take a backseat, he may very well leave. If that happens, perhaps some of those leadership qualities you saw in him weren't as deeply rooted as you thought.

In most of the similar client situations I've witnessed, Bobby usually appreciates the open and honest conversations about the potential you see in him, as well as your need to bring in experienced leadership to fuel the company's growth. It's important that you show Bobby your appreciation. Most people in this situation want to feel like their hard work and dedication was worth it. And isn't this what made Bobby such a critical B-player in the first place?

B-Players Are People Too!

If it isn't yet clear, there are a number of people who might be considered B-players in your world. And there are a number of archetypes to be on the lookout for. In the right seats in the right company, B-players can be great! Many are solid performers who get their jobs done with no drama. Don't discount their worth as solid team members and productive individual contributors.

But B-players usually stop being solid performers when pushed beyond their limits. In some cases, they'll compensate for their shortcomings; in others, they'll do whatever it takes to hide those shortcomings from you. In the worst cases, they crash and burn and end up costing the company a boatload of time, money, and heartache!

One of my own shortcomings is that I think everyone has A-player potential hidden inside them. Of course, you know that's simply not true. Over the years, I've learned the hard way that not everyone has "it" or even wants "it." That's one of the reasons I brought on my execution partner, Next-Level Natalie (chapters 11 and 12) and stopped worrying about hiring and whether someone has potential. Since then, I haven't promoted anyone out of loyalty, fear of losing them, or my own stupidity!

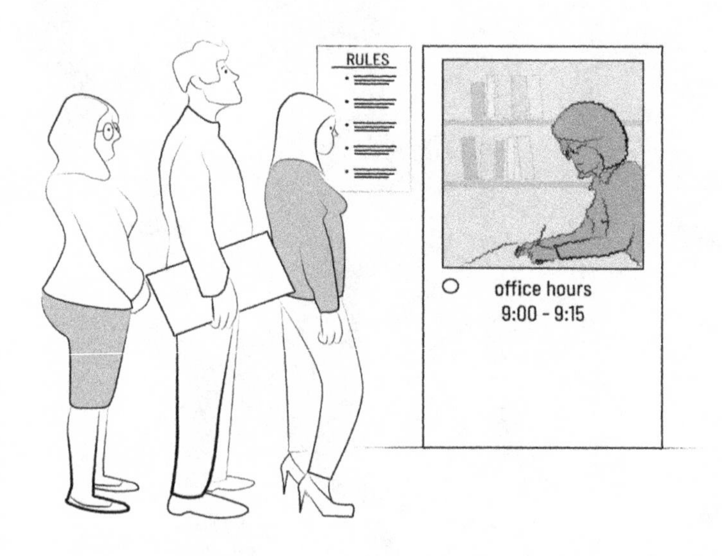
RULES
office hours
9:00 - 9:15

10

HR RHODA

WHY WE HATE HUMAN RESOURCES

"We repositioned our tactical and reactive HR organization to a more proactive Employee Experience function. We now support our employees with a full end-to-end experience. Creating an amazing employee experience for their woom journey is a key differentiator in attracting talent to woom. Without it we'd be dead with the competition for talent in today's market and our team wouldn't be a high performance one."

– **Mathias Ihlenfeld,** woom bikes CEO

Most entrepreneurs hate human resources (source: VIRTUALLY EVERY ENTREPRENEUR I'VE EVER MET). I find it rather ironic that the individuals in your company who are supposed to be focused on people are often the most frustrating part of the organization—for your people. Why is that?

The term "human resources" has been around since John Commons's 1893 book, *The Distribution of Wealth.*[7] It's the kind of term that everyone has heard, and most of us have an idea of what it is. But what does it really mean? The answer to this question varies from company to company, but the answer likely depends on whether the company has over fifty employees, because that's when most federal compliance laws kick in.

Ugh, compliance. That's what most entrepreneurs think of when they hear the term "human resources." If you ask ten entrepreneurs what they think about "human resources," you're likely to get ten versions of "Dammit! Let's talk about something else." Admit it—you had a queasy feeling in your stomach and almost skipped this chapter when you saw HR in the title, didn't you?

Your frustration with HR is likely related to the following reality:

The HR department for emerging companies typically has approximately fifteen to twenty responsibilities, of which there are twelve to fifteen they can get fired for if they goof them up: things like payroll, payroll taxes, benefits, compliance, state regulations, etc.

Meanwhile, the four or five areas you find aspirational take a backseat because they tend to feel like they're nice-to-haves and not have-to-haves. For most emerging companies, your HR team simply doesn't know how to make them happen! Things like culture, recruiting A-players, training and development, and employee engagement become afterthoughts. As a result, most HR professionals at entrepreneurial companies tend to gravitate toward compliance and tactics.

This is why taskmasters thrive in this role, while the "people" people, strategists, and culture builders don't make it at emerging companies; partially because they're expensive, and partially because they're generally not detail-oriented. This explains why you think many of the HR folks you've worked with at emerging companies are HR wonks—and you have little respect for them.

You're not alone. The reality is we all have HR nightmares, but it doesn't have to be that way! A good HR or people function can be a key unlocking move as you scale your company. But I believe it requires two different skill sets. One is more strategic and helps you build the organization of your dreams: a purpose-driven company with a great culture that attracts, retains, and develops top talent. The second is more tactical and allows you to rest easy: confident that the more compliance-related tasks are handled—the things that'll keep you out of court, out of jail, and off the evening news.

Unfortunately, most entrepreneurs don't see the people function as a strategic part of the company; they only see the tactical, compliance-related part and think of it as a necessary evil. Which is how most of us end up with HR Rhoda and why we hate HR. And the vicious cycle continues.

Meet HR Rhoda and Human Resources Rod

The Taskmaster

While we may not appreciate it as entrepreneurs, our companies need the tactical HR role. We need someone to ensure the team's paid on time, to handle workplace-related issues, to research employee benefits, and to ensure compliance with the mountain of rules required by federal, state, and local governmental agencies. Unfortunately, this is the price of doing business and has to get done.

That's one version of HR Rhoda: a taskmaster who's driven to ensure all the i's are dotted and t's are crossed. She's great at the details—but not so great with the H in HR. In fact, she might be one of the least-liked people in the office. It doesn't help that she locks herself and her precious personnel files and payroll records in her office all day or that most employees feel like anything they share with Rhoda ends up in her weekly report to the CEO. So literally, the worst people person in the company is often charged with the people aspect!

Rhoda may have started on the accounting team or as an administrative assistant, or she may have been one of your generalists like Bounce-Around Betty. But as the company grew, the need for HR became evident. She did some research and determined HR was a path for career growth. She took some classes online and immersed herself in certifications with cool titles like APHR, APTD, and SPHR that looked good on paper. Let's face it, it's not an easy job, but there's a low barrier to entry. You don't have to know how to develop code or design bridges to cut payroll checks on time!

Honestly, it doesn't really matter how Rhoda gets to you, as long as she's competent. She's great with details. She highlights the signature lines on paperwork, informs employees about open enrollment, and handles their questions without breaking a sweat. You sleep well knowing that payroll is on time, administrative tasks are handled, and the government is satisfied. But you want more from HR. You want a talent strategy, a great place to work, a cause for people to believe in.

Human Resources Rod: A Different Version

Another version we might see with entrepreneurial companies is Human Resources Rod, who is everything Rhoda's not. He's an outgoing people person who espouses the company culture. In fact, you've often called him your culture champion. "If only we had more Rods . . ." you'd say.

Rod was on your operations team before you plucked him out of there to take on HR. You were bound and determined not to neglect the "human" side of human resources, so you convinced him to take the role. Unfortunately, Rod's not so great at details—which is kind of important, especially when payroll taxes are underreported and the Feds get involved (I've seen it). He's not the best person for this role in the traditional sense.

There are certainly plenty of Rods out there. We also see quite a few wannabe counselors. You know the type: they're great at employee relations, spending most of their time consoling emotionally dysfunctional employees. Tasks don't get done, nor does strategy, just a bunch of talking. For this chapter we're going to focus on the HR Rhodas of the world, the taskmasters, mainly because this is the most common archetype assuming this role for entrepreneurial companies.

Why We Hate HR

In the opening paragraph, I quoted my source on the hate for HR, as "virtually every entrepreneur I've ever met." If you want something more scientific, it doesn't take much more than a simple Google search to find countless others who agree, including articles like *Harvard Business Review*'s

"Why We Love to Hate HR" and *Forbes*'s "Ten Reasons Everybody Hates HR."[8]

I want to ask a deeper why: Why, or how, did we reach this point? I don't think people get into HR to become compliance nitpickers. They get into HR because they have a passion for people. Then they get sucked into the administrative burdens required of the profession—like teachers, who get into teaching because they have a passion for inspiring students but get their energy zapped by the mountains of tasks required of teachers, ultimately losing their passion for teaching. Other examples include doctors who got into healthcare to help patients, or police who got into law enforcement to protect citizens, only to lose their zest for their chosen field because of bureaucracy and paperwork.

I think the same thing happened in HR. There are just so many rules and regulations around payroll and employment law (ever hired an employee in California?) and the mindset has become so much about protecting the company that HR just got sucked into that mindset. They're so fearful of making mistakes that they have to be rigid about compliance. You're frustrated because you're asking them to "please think outside the box on this" while HR is saying, "How can I think outside the box when you're also telling me to follow every rule?"

By the end of 2021, HR had spent most of the previous two years trying to figure out CDC COVID-19 compliance and how to put arrows on the carpet so people can walk and maintain social distancing. Do we also expect them to have time to create a training and development plan?

Question: Is HR a vicious cycle? We're so frustrated with "typical" HR and our disrespect of the position that we don't invest much salary, resources, and effort into attracting stellar candidates. We get what we pay for, and we become even more frustrated with HR. And on and on . . .

What Got You Here Won't Get You There

When your company started out, you and your inner circle set the culture—good, bad, or indifferent. You didn't need an official mission statement or even a plan. You set the culture by living, breathing, and leading—your way! No matter whether you're a command-and-control leader, a laid-back, team-meetings-at-the-yoga-studio guy, or if you're a leader who builds teams to rally together and take on the world, you're setting the culture.

Back then, you knew everyone, either because you hired them yourself or because your team included college buddies, relatives, or neighbors. You knew how they fit into what you were doing. Mike might not have been the best accountant, but he damn sure worked hard! And when your team was small, they knew each other and could interact with you 24/7—whether it was critical work issues or last night's game. Culture "stuff" happened naturally.

But what happens when your team grows to thirty, forty, or fifty people? The business is complicated, and growth is chaotic. Can you really maintain a personal connection with everyone? The good news is: this is a natural part of growth. Once you hit a certain point (typically between thirty and fifty employees), your culture will need to shift from personal connection with you to something more scalable—starting with your purpose, vision, and values.

What We Want Versus What We Get

Your Dreams

Many of us aspire to do much more than "blocking and tackling" when it comes to people. You're envious of other companies with amazing cultures who're getting recognized as Best Places to Work. If you're part of a CEO organization like YPO, Vistage, EO, or countless others, you've seen or heard of other leaders with great, almost idyllic cultures—you want some of that.

For me, it was the Stagen Integral Leadership Program (ILP) that opened my eyes to what culture could do for my company. I saw my peers apparently building amazing teams around a shared purpose, with everything emanating from the founder's vision. And yes, I wanted that!

> **Side Note**: Be careful comparing yourself to your peers—especially their highlight reel. FOMO is real and is a problem for many of us in YPO, Vistage, Stagen, etc. Not everyone (or anyone, really) has their shit together like they want you to believe in these settings or how they portray themselves on social media.

The key to accomplishing this goal isn't a superhero founder who somehow knows every employee intimately, leads team-building exercises, and creates a Pollyanna atmosphere. Like most of the characters in this book, it's important to recognize where you need help, and to partner with people stronger than you to reach your goals!

Enter Rhoda

Many of us want Rhoda to create the amazing culture we're seeking. I mean, over the years, she handled our day-to-day, tactical HR so well that we don't even think about them. She says she can handle more responsibilities and relishes the challenge of partnering with you to build strategic HR.

Those of you who have tried placing Rhoda in the more strategic role usually become frustrated when she isn't able to magically become your strategic talent partner. Instead of being frustrated, we should be thanking Rhoda for all she's done for the organization, including keeping us out of legal trouble and making sure payroll is paid accurately and on time.

In some cases, Rhoda might have the potential to develop into a next-level talent partner who can help document your purpose, vision, and values and then develop a talent strategy aligned with them. But usually, your tactical HR team isn't what you're looking for in a talent partner—at least not at this stage of their career and your company's growth.

Tactical generalists rarely make good talent strategists and partners for entrepreneurs. It's possible that Rhoda can grow into the role—but she's going to need coaching and she'll learn a lot of lessons the hard way as she grows.

She'll also need to offload the tactical HR to someone else. If not, she'll always wrestle with the same compliance-related push-pull we mentioned many times before.

It's Not a One-Man Show

No matter how you define it, I believe the people function for emerging companies requires two different skill sets. And you don't usually find someone with both. Even if you did, there's not enough time in the day! There are usually enough tactical duties to keep someone busy full time. You can't afford to put strategy on the back burner while you wait for open enrollment to close!

At the end of this chapter we'll discuss a few ways to make this work and how to pay for it. Having both strategic "people operations" and tactical "traditional HR" working well together is magical.

Side Note: I've always thought of the two roles as (1) someone focusing on administration and compliance; and (2) someone focusing on strategy, culture, and people. But my friend Chris Allen gave me another way to look at it—one person focused on protection, and another focused on attraction. The attraction person becomes more of the strategic leader who leads recruiting, development, and training as "chief people officer," while the "traditional" HR, or protection position, is a role under that umbrella.

To Chris's point: Many companies have HR report up to legal counsel or the CFO in order to protect the company. And most schooling and development for HR professionals is about protecting the company. In numerous conversations over the years, HR leaders have lamented something like, "When I'm talking to employees, I find my mind drifting away from the conversation and toward protecting the assets of the company. That's not right."

Real-World Example

The First Hire

When he started out, my friend Curtis hired mostly people he knew. An accountant from church, an operations guy he drank beer with—you know the drill by now. For HR, he wanted someone with people skills. He'd had too many run-ins with HR types in the past who seemed to hate their job!

So Curtis actually hired his kid's manny, Rod, to be his first HR hire. You read that right—their manny. In his defense, he was great with people, had a good head on his shoulders, and had a promising future. At first he was pretty solid. The team loved him and he created an onboarding program that made employees feel welcome from day one. But he SUCKED at the tactical items. Benefits were nonexistent, payroll was always an adventure, and he couldn't seem to get organized.

Upgrade Attempt

Curtis decided to make a change—and upgrade. He desperately wanted to build an award-winning culture, a company that stood for something and made an impact in the community. He was inspired at a Scaling Up Summit by the stories of fellow attendees and the impactful cultures they had apparently created at their companies. He wanted to brag about HIS company's culture. So he set off to upgrade the HR position.

But Curtis didn't realize how expensive strategic people leadership was. He couldn't possibly justify spending THAT much. So, he did what many entrepreneurs do—he didn't upgrade, he settled! He hired Rhoda, a career HR professional he could afford. She had lots of fancy letters after her name, and she definitely said the right things about building a great culture.

Unfortunately, she wasn't able to do what Curtis envisioned. She had not done the strategic work before, so she ended up doing what most HR generalists do—she focused on the things she was comfortable doing and those that would get her fired if they fell through the cracks. And she was damn good at them!

Sure, Curtis needed those things done, but he wanted a culture of attraction. He wanted someone to push his company to new heights, but he ended up with a tactical guru who followed the rules. It's hard to blame Rhoda. She simply followed the blueprint created by the HR profession.

Finally Got It Right

Curtis was frustrated again, and this time threw the budget out the window. He knew he would pay a lot for the right person, but he was willing to pay whatever it took this time. He needed a culture strategy, and a talent roadmap with hiring, onboarding, training, and development plans.

He ended up partnering with an experienced chief people officer who helped him: first with a ninety-day project to build the foundation and then on an ongoing, fractional basis. Rhoda stayed on to handle the tactical HR role—and she's on fire! She's witnessing first-hand how to build a strategic people initiative and she's getting the coaching and mentoring needed to advance her career. Will she be able to move from tactical to strategic? Only time will tell. While very rare, it can happen.

The Path Forward

As an entrepreneur, you want your culture to be more than just a placard on the wall, more than the typical bullshit mission statement many of us see right through. You want your company to stand for something and for your core values to be how you hire, fire, and evaluate performance. This is hard to do on your own. You need help!

That help comes in the form of strategic people operations and tactical (traditional) HR. If you're a big company with deep pockets, maybe you can afford an HR generalist AND a chief people officer. But most of us don't have that luxury—at least not at first.

Like Curtis, I often see entrepreneurs make a mistake by settling. They set out to hire a Rockstar culture guru and later realize they don't want to shell out $150k–$250k annually for that level of person. So they end up settling for another HR generalist and the cycle of frustration continues! In fact, right now you're probably shouting, "250 grand?! Holy smokes!"

Luckily, there are some creative options out there. One is to outsource your entire HR function to a third-party firm: not a bad idea. There are plenty out there and I've seen some have success with this. But most of the time it seems like that firm's strategic leaders are spread too thin across clients to devote enough time to your company. Sure, you get plenty of time from the tactical HR team—but that's not where you want help!

One of the more exciting developments in the entrepreneurial community is a fractional chief people (or talent) officer. The right person works on a part-time basis to bring your vision to life. This person works with you to develop clarity and alignment around purpose, vision, and values, create a long-term talent strategy, and develop a plan to attract and retain game-changing talent.

In those cases where you think Rhoda may be well-suited to develop into a strategic role over time, there's an added benefit to this role. Rhoda can learn from and be coached and mentored by the right fractional leader. However, it's important that someone inside the company own the culture and people strategy. I encourage the CEO to own it but leverage this fractional CPO as your execution partner. Meanwhile, project management for much of this could be a great role for Rhoda!

There are a number of service providers out there (including HireBetter) that help the leaders of emerging companies with this chief people officer initiative. These firms can either serve in that role as a consulting firm or help the CEO identify an individual to do so. Experienced eyes from the outside can develop a plan to bring your culture vision to life.

Whatever path you choose, make sure you identify someone who has developed people before and been part of building a company similar to yours in size and rate of growth. And, of course, you'll want them to be more people-focused than task-focused.

People Are People Too!

As I mentioned in the beginning of this chapter, "human resources" is an accepted business term, but why? People shouldn't be "resources." Some companies proclaim, "people are our most important asset." Why "asset"? Accountants know that assets depreciate over time, but people don't depreciate. In fact, they actually increase in value if we invest in them. Borrowing again from Chris Allen—the new language should be, "People are our greatest investment."

We invest in things we believe will increase in value. Creating an intentional culture that meets human needs and connects people to intrinsic motivation will see people thrive. When we really believe in an investment, we'll even double down!

The HR industry now uses terms like "Human Capital" or "People Operations," but changing titles doesn't change the way a person or department operates. The truth is, HR doesn't have to suck, and it should be one of your company's strongest departments, but changing the name isn't enough.

The real problem with HR is rooted in the way we think about it. Entrepreneurs see companies with great culture, vision, and a knack for attracting and retaining talent, and they say, "THAT'S what my HR person should be doing!" But in almost every entrepreneurial company, HR generalists simply aren't cut out for that type of work. Next-level planning, culture building, and talent strategy aren't in the wheelhouse of someone who's spent years running compliance.

For more on creating an intentional culture and inspiring a team of motivated employees, check out Intermission III, Building a Great Culture.

INTERMISSION III

BUILDING A GREAT CULTURE

"Teamwork is the ability to work together toward a common vision. The ability to direct individual accomplishments toward organizational objectives. It is the fuel that allows common people to attain uncommon results."

— Widely attributed to Andrew Carnegie

So far, we've covered a host of characters you're likely to meet on your entrepreneurial journey. I've provided some warning signs for folks like Pipeline Paul and Resume Ralph, given some pointers for dealing with legacy employees like Bounce-Around Betty and Right-Hand Rita, and even encouraged you to find ways to put your Harrys and Mikes in the best position to succeed. Now let's talk about putting all the pieces together.

You want to "get the right people on the bus . . . in the right seats, and the wrong people off the bus," like Jim Collins, acclaimed author of *Good to Great*, says.[9] And since you want to build a great TEAM, it doesn't matter how talented they are individually if they don't work together toward a common vision. I've seen some "teams" comprised of very talented individuals (in business and in sports) implode when leadership was unable to build a culture of "we" over "me." When everyone's working together—toward a shared vision, with a shared purpose and shared values—you've got a recipe for success. You're building a winning culture. And a winning team.

Building Your Culture

What makes your company special? Why would an A-player decide to leave their current company to come work for yours? What motivates your team to succeed? Do you, as the leader, inspire greatness in the team around you? If you don't have clear answers to these questions and many more like them, you've got some work to do.

People's views about employment are changing. Times are different now than they were twenty years ago—hell, times are different than they were twenty months ago, pre-pandemic! This is especially true for Millennial and Gen Z employees, but it's becoming commonplace in older generations in the workforce, as well. People crave PURPOSE: something to believe in—something to fight for.

Exchanging forty hours a week simply for a paycheck is not cutting it anymore. It's not satisfying the craving for belonging. The wave has been coming and is now a tsunami. In a 2021 *Fortune* article, the percentage of people with jobs who were looking for a new one steadily increased for ten years—until 2021 when the number spiked to 65 percent of US workers.[10] And yes, COVID-19 exacerbated the problem, but it just produced a spike in what was already happening.

People Want to Be Fulfilled—At Home *and* at Work

As a leader, it's up to you to create an environment people want to be a part of. A great culture doesn't magically happen, either. Like most things worth having, it ain't easy. And, at the risk of sounding like a broken record, there's no one-size-fits-all solution for building a great culture. So much depends on your industry, your leadership style, and what matters to you and your team. Yet the bottom line is still the same: without a strong culture, vision, purpose, and sense of community, your company will not reach its full potential.

The Value of a Great Culture

Think about every group you've ever been part of: from hanging with your buddies on the elementary school playground, to your college social club, to your weekly Bible study group, to the fellow parents in the stands at your kids' baseball field. What binds those groups together? What is it that takes a group of random people and turns them into a community?

The answer is . . . shared values.

In second grade, my values were to have fun playing tag and tackle-the-man-with-the-ball. In college, it was connections and people to experience college with, and faith is the connection for Bible study groups. High school friends share a coming of age (and heated debates about who WAS the better athlete and who NOW cooks up the best crawfish boils). In youth sports, it's all about supporting our kids as they compete in their sport of choice.

If there were no shared values, there'd be no community. This spans the spectrum—from countries, states, cities, special-interest groups, and volunteer organizations, all the way down to individual relationships between people. Shared values are at the core.

I thought this was a business book. Why are we talking about community?

First of all, I hope this book is the antithesis of every business book you've ever read! Second, values are what bring groups together in the business world too. Entrepreneurs launch their business around a vision of what can be. In order to reach that goal, others need to buy in. That vision is shared with them—and they either become part of the community or leave the company.

Early on, that was easy; the entrepreneur was available every day for everyone in the company. Your employees became your friends if they weren't already. The entrepreneur's values were easily conveyed to the rest of the team because they regularly saw you in action.

But as your company grows and you become less available to every employee, it becomes harder for him or her to be the culture czar for the organization. It's important that the organization develops into a community so that the core values are bigger than and outlive the entrepreneur.

How do I create an amazing culture when I'm already busting my ass just to build this company?

First of all, as you'll read below, the company will be much more successful if you have a strong team than if the founder is a superhero. Secondly, as your team grows, it's hard to maintain the connection you used to have with everyone. In fact, I'd argue that shared values happen naturally when you're in the foxhole together, scratching and clawing to survive. But it's harder to create that same camaraderie with the new accountant or sales rep who wasn't there by your side.

Honestly, you shouldn't try this on your own. With HR Rhoda, we talked about the concept of the chief people officer or even the fractional people officer. Now might be the time to seek help, but not from your tactical HR person—they're not thinking about creating community, they're thinking about executing payroll. In order to become a world-class team, they need something to believe in, something to work toward. You'll be a much stronger company when you make this happen.

I've heard a lot about core values and culture. Honestly, it feels soft. Can't I just pay them more to make them happy?

No! As I said before, money isn't the only motivator for employees anymore. There are exceptions, but the people you want on your team want purpose in their lives. They want to be fulfilled. They want what they do to matter. It's not just about holidays, weekends, and retirement. You've got to offer more than just a paycheck to attract, retain, and motivate the best employees!

Money is still important; but more credence is given to purpose and shared values these days.

Uncovering Your Purpose

A purpose-driven team provides a sense of belonging and fulfillment that's bigger than its members. Purpose can turn a good team into a great one. Great cultures include a purpose the team can rally behind and core values that drive them. But they have to be real. You can't just slap slogans and photos on a wall and expect a great culture. Building culture takes time, dedication, and lots of repetition!

> Warren Bennis, who was widely considered to be at the forefront of authentic leadership, summarized our need for purpose in "The Secret of Great Groups," published in *Leader to Leader*: "All great teams—and all great organizations—are built around a shared dream or motivating purpose. Yet . . . mission statements often lack real meaning and resonance. Realistically, your team need not believe that it is literally saving the world; it is enough to feel it is helping people in need or battling a tough competitor. Simply punching a time clock doesn't do it. Articulating a meaningful mission is the job of leaders at every level—and it's not an easy task."[11]

How do I create my company's purpose?

You don't necessarily "create" purpose. I believe it should be uncovered. Ask your team, "What would be lost if our company went away? Why is it important that we continue to exist?" Press them on their answers until the reason for the company's existence becomes clear. This is sometimes called the "five whys" technique, originally developed by Sakichi Toyoda, founder of Toyota.

This process sounds simple, but that doesn't mean it's easy. Some organizations take months or even years to clarify their purpose. But the end result is worth its weight in gold because everything you do hereafter will emanate from your purpose.

When I took over HireBetter, one of the issues we identified was a lack of clarity around what we were trying to accomplish. HireBetter was a recruiting firm, yes, so we were connecting great candidates with aspirational companies. That's all good, but what was it that separated HireBetter from the thousands of other companies that claim to do that too?

For us, it was asking each other, "Why?" The team was so passionate about the impact we have on people's lives that we knew it had to be more powerful than simply "placing successful candidates with great companies." And they sure wanted to be way more than just a transactional middleman, which is so prevalent in the recruiting industry. So we honed, and we asked why, and we asked why, and we honed again. Eventually, we landed on our purpose, which we call our impact statement: "*We impact lives by connecting and empowering good people to build great companies.*"

We work with good people. The "No Asshole" policy is in full effect. We connect them to each other and empower them to do great things. This includes everyone around us—our team, candidates with whom we work, and the leaders of companies who partner with us. It's more than recruiting; it's helping good people (good-hearted, good-souled people) build something special. Hell, it's why I'm writing this book!

I don't know . . . it still sounds daunting.

Just ask yourself, "Why?" Keep asking until it becomes clear. Look, the recruiting industry is broken, so I was starting at a deficit. But we've built something special that truly impacts lives in a positive way. No matter what industry you're in, what product you sell, or what service you provide, your purpose is in there somewhere, begging to come out. Sometimes what you do makes this obvious. If you sell Kevlar vests that protect our troops in war zones, that's a pretty easy purpose to rally behind—or if your company develops systems to keep hospitals running.

What about me? I sell dry-cleaning chemicals . . .

Even if you don't have a crystal-clear, can-be-seen-from-outer-space-it's-so-obvious purpose, you still have one. If you sell dry-cleaning solutions, for example, your purpose is probably customer-oriented. You want to provide quality solutions so people's clothes can be cleaned effectively and safely, with an affordable price tag—so they'll look their best on the job interview or on date night.

Spoiler alert: Your purpose doesn't have to be "save the world." In fact, very few companies can claim that as their purpose. Finding your purpose isn't about exaggerating your importance or projecting some false narrative about what you do. It's about highlighting the "why" behind your work and making that the rock, the foundation, for everything you do.

OK, I'm starting to understand. I think "service-oriented" is something I can get behind!

Yes! Businesses exist to serve a particular need within a community. By having a service-oriented approach, you're setting a tone that your business cares about other peoples' needs and desires. This approach can work for every company, from a fast-food chain to an investment banking firm.

My good friend Amy Porter, founder of AffiniPay (a very successful company that creates industry-specific online payment tools), shared with me their mantra: "put customers first and success comes after." That's easy to say, but how does that translate day-to-day? One of AffiniPay's core values is to be "surprisingly great," meaning they want to create experiences that exceed expectations. It could be as simple as answering the phone on the first ring, responding to an email right away, or following up with a customer. Her team finds it FUN to create new ways to beat expectations!

Living Your Values

When AffiniPay made the decision to put customers first and maniacally focus on service, their work was just beginning. Being purpose-driven means that you not only have a clear purpose and values, but you put those into practice in everything you do. Your core values aren't just words on a T-shirt. They should influence how you hire, fire, and promote. It goes way beyond people too. They should be the rock upon which every major decision is made, the clients you accept, the awards you apply for, and how you engage in the community.

This isn't easy! You might find the pull of the almighty dollar too strong to pass up at times, especially when you're negotiating with a major customer, acquiring a company, or selling yours. But if the team buys into the culture and owns the process, they'll be holding YOU accountable! I love it when my team spouts off core values or our impact statement. It's so much more powerful when they own it—versus a top-down approach.

A Few Examples

Goals are what we want to achieve, but values are what we think is important. If your company doesn't have a well-defined purpose operating under a well-known set of values that the team can rally around, you'll face challenges. From employees not knowing their limits, to losing key employees, to internal squabbling—cracks will form. I've seen companies where rules were loosey-goosey and team members didn't feel supported. Turnover was rampant and the company was in chaos.

Uncertainty may have ruled the day when you started out, but now that you're trying to scale this puppy, you need stability; you need order.

That stability and direction comes from harnessing the "why" behind what you do and building a culture that'll do whatever it takes to make it happen. When a company rallies around a purpose, it can be magical. Here are a few examples:

People-First: A people-centric culture places profits second and focuses on the team first and foremost. Employees are more committed, they're more productive, and they take more ownership when they feel more important to leadership than profit margins. Ironically, when I've been around people-centric cultures, the team works harder to serve customers, who are willing to pay more for services and are more loyal to the company—which increases profitability. A team of servant leaders working well together succeeds or fails as a team, and they're more loyal to each other and the company. When you put your people first, satisfied customers and company success will follow.

Growth: I've worked with a number of companies who make growth their mantra. The ones who just want to grow financially don't remain clients for long, because we want to work with companies that stand for more. For many companies, though, growth is also about the personal and professional growth of the members of the team: everyone from the CEO to the entry-level new hire. Growth-oriented cultures are fun to be around. Employees are encouraged and given opportunities to develop professionally, new hires are sought out based on their desire to grow, and the team is motivated and empowered to help the COMPANY grow.

Transparency: For most of us, this sounds terrifying! Leading with transparency means you're trusting the team with your highs AND lows. You believe in the team so much that you know they can handle all information, good and bad. If done right, this encourages the team to engage in creative and proactive problem-solving across the organization. My friend Mason Ayer at Kerbey Lane Café in Austin runs his business as an open book—and the team, at all levels, is consistently stepping up to improve operational efficiencies.

When COVID-19 shut down the economy in 2020, companies who valued transparency were able to shift gears quickly—collaborating and solving complex problems were already in their DNA. One such company, Aceable, was transparent around financial performance and products they were developing, and why. In March 2020, when the shit hit the fan, leadership shared their concerns with their 200 employees. This empowered the team to proactively solve problems and cut costs. When the dust settled on 2020, they actually BEAT their original income projections for the year!

Profit: You don't need a transparent or make-the-world-a-better-place approach in order to build an amazing culture. It's absolutely OK to make maximizing profits your culture! There are some amazing companies out there who exist to maximize profits for shareholders and employees. Some tie that into the work they do—like an investment advisor, for example. Their goal is to maximize profits for customers, which is service-oriented.

But others are less feel-good. Many employees are driven by paychecks, they're goal-oriented, and want to make money for the company and its shareholders so that THEY make more money. They thrive in environments where quantitative analysis and metrics-driven decision-making are king. Just make sure you're upfront about this being your culture. Like all other cultural decisions, some people won't be on board (and that's OK!).

Bringing It Home

Building a winning culture that people want to be a part of isn't easy! But you'll be well on your way once you identify:

1. Your purpose—why you exist
2. Your vision—what you are trying to accomplish
3. Your core values—what you think is important

As your company evolves, you'll find that your team will become stronger, smarter, and more agile as they focus on these concepts. But it doesn't stop with the team! If your team knows where it's going, knows why it exists, and knows its guiding principles, you'll be a better leader. Because your company will have buy-in at every level—and that, my friends, is a great culture.

"In leading people, take a page from parenting. Establish a handful of rules, repeat yourself a lot, and act consistently with those rules. This is the role of and power of Core Values. If discovered and used effectively, these values guide all the relationship decisions and systems in the company."

– **Verne Harnish** in his
bestseller *Scaling Up*.[12]

11

NEXT-LEVEL NATALIE (PART 1)

YOUR OPERATING PARTNER

"Visionary entrepreneurs have powerful natural gifts that make them unique. When focused, they can lead to tremendous organizational success. You're at your Visionary best when you leverage those gifts by joining forces with an Integrator who takes on the role of making your ideas actually happen. A strong Integrator can execute your vision, make it a reality, and propel your business to new heights."

– **Mark C. Winters,** Co-Author of *Rocket Fuel*

In previous chapters, we explored the types of people you'll encounter on your entrepreneurial journey. Some of the characters we've met are solid employees who just need to be given the right direction, the right role, or the right tools. Some are quite the opposite; worthless may be too strong a word, but it's directionally accurate. The reality for entrepreneurial companies is that, in order to build a great team, you're going to make some mistakes along the way.

Now let's talk about the keystone character: the leader who can bring it all together, put the right people in the right seats; the missing piece of the puzzle that will help us live up to our potential. The next two chapters and intermission will focus on this keystone character. In this chapter I'll outline the need and set the stage, the Intermission will include tips on identifying, recruiting, and onboarding, and chapter 12 will cover working together to build the company of your dreams. And I'll share the good, the bad, and the ugly of my own experiences with this magical character.

First, let's set the stage. Most entrepreneurs have big ideas—lots of them. We're strategic thinkers and culture champions, we're great with key relationships and closing big deals, or maybe we're tech whizzes or product development dynamos. In their cult hit and guidebook for entrepreneurial companies, *Rocket Fuel*, Mark Winters and Gino Wickman call this person the "Visionary."[13] (More on that later.) The key point is, as great as we are with big-picture stuff, we're not so good at holding people accountable, managing the day-to-day, following through, or details. Sound familiar?

The Problem

In a startup, you need that kind of leadership—someone with passion and vision who can inspire the team to greatness. Those early days rely on the entrepreneur and the heroic efforts of a few employees. As we discussed in earlier chapters, this is the golden age of the generalists, people who will do anything and everything: fun times for those of us who thrive on chaos!

But as your organization grows, things need to change. The whack-a-mole style of management won't work if you're attempting to scale, if you're trying to build a successful company that's bigger than you. It's time to move from fighting fires to fire prevention by building the infrastructure to scale the business. It's time to make some key moves to take your company to the next level.

Here's the hard truth, which actually might come as a relief: you're probably not the one to lead those efforts. Sure, there are exceptions. Some entrepreneurs are solid operators, but most of us aren't. We thrive on chaos and aren't built for systems, processes, structure, and rules.

I get it—I'm one of you! I realize all that stuff is necessary if we're going to build a great company. I just don't know how to do it. I mean, I suck at details. And processes. And rules. To be honest, I don't WANT to be good at it. I'm just not wired that way. Give me someone I can partner with to do all that foundational stuff that I know is necessary, just not any fun (for me, at least).

What Should You Be Doing? What COULD You Be Doing?

If you've read any entrepreneurial musings over the past twenty-five years, you've probably heard the following phrase a thousand times: "*As a leader, you need to be working ON your business, not IN your business.*" But what does that really mean?

Well, for starters, as CEO you shouldn't be involved in the day-to-day operations of your company. You're probably not good at those things anyway. "Not me, Kurt," you might retort. "I can do it!" Maybe you can, but is that where you should be spending your time? And if you're anything like me, you hate the day-to-day grind that—if you could—you'd never do again.

Question: What if you could surround yourself with great employees and experienced leaders, so you can leave all the day-to-day behind and focus not only on what you love doing but what you're great at? Think of how good things would be, what a huge unlocking move it would be for you.

So what are you good at? What are you passionate about? What things should you be focusing on? Answering those questions will be huge for you. There are tools and resources out there like *StrengthsFinder* and *StrengthsFinder 2.0* by Tom Rathman and the accompanying StrengthsFinder assessment by Don Clifton to help you figure out . . . well, your strengths. I've taken the assessment and I also took part in Stagen's ILP Program to help me uncover my purpose, which I highly recommend.

Let's get personal. How are you doing when it comes to doing the things you're good at, you love to do, and only you can do?

> My good friend Rod Kurtz—a longtime business journalist, founder of a successful media strategy firm, and Entrepreneur-in-Residence at UCLA's Anderson School of Management—shared with me a simple but effective exercise to help determine where you should be spending your time. Note that other versions of this exercise can be found in almost any leadership or productivity book out there. I happen to like this one the best.

Get out a pad of sticky notes and on a piece of paper, draw four quadrants and label them 1 through 4. Now use those sticky notes and quadrants to make four lists:

1. Things I'm good at
2. Things I like doing
3. Things I'm bad at
4. Things I hate doing

On the sticky notes, write down as many of the things you do as possible—one item per note. Once you have an exhaustive list, place the notes in each of the quadrants. Be brutally honest. What are you really good at that only you can do for the company? What do you enjoy doing that you'd miss if someone else took it over? What are you bogged down by that you're not even good at? What makes you dread coming to work—at your own freakin' company, no less?

Obviously, the goal here is to eliminate the things you're bad at and things you hate doing. Ask yourself why you're still doing those things. These two negative lists will help determine what skills you need to augment by adding another employee or an operating partner.

Once you realize your need to focus on your strengths and mitigate your weaknesses with other people, you're halfway there. And if you're able to bring in the right person to partner with—and you work well together—now you're cooking with gas, as we say in the South!

Introducing Next-Level Natalie

Next-Level Natalie is the kind of person who lives and breathes execution, operations, and getting things done. Her mind works on a totally different level than most entrepreneurs. She's able to understand your vision AND see all the moving parts needed to make it a reality. Put simply—she completes you. She's the yin to your yang, the peanut butter to your jelly, the hot dog to your bun.

When you have an idea, Natalie can break down what it'll take to make it happen and help you prioritize that idea against all your other ideas, while balancing the company's other initiatives. And if she's really good, has your respect, and has institutional backing, she can tell you if your idea is: (a) great and needs to be implemented right away; (b) solid but should be further down the list of priorities; or (c) a complete waste of time!

I'm a classic Visionary as defined in *Rocket Fuel*, and I believe most of my fellow entrepreneurs fall into the Visionary bucket. I'll be honest—I have the potential to be scattered and all over the place. I do have some great ideas (and a lot of harebrained ones too!) and a vision for the organization. But what people like me need is a #2, a partner who can turn that vision into a reality: someone to develop an execution plan, hire the right people, and hold them accountable.

Next-Level Natalie goes by a number of titles. Chief operating officer, president, or partner are commonly used. I've seen some Natalies with the CEO title, including mine! (More on that in chapter 12.) The use of the Integrator title is gaining traction (pun intended) thanks to *Rocket Fuel* and other books in the *Traction* series by Gino Wickman (more on that in Intermission IV).[14]

If you're not familiar with the Integrator concept, I often describe this person as the entrepreneur's execution partner or operating partner. I use these terms interchangeably, but no matter what name or title you give Natalie, here is how I describe her function:

- Natalie's your execution partner.
- She brings organizational clarity to your vision and orients the team toward it.
- She develops a roadmap to accomplish it and works with you to establish goals and key initiatives to attain those goals.
- She establishes annual budgets and cascades the company's goals and objectives down to departmental and individual goals, metrics, and incentives.
- She distills the company's long-term goals into annual, quarterly, and monthly goals that are actionable, measurable, and easy to understand.
- She brings a new level of accountability that, for most entrepreneurs, is missing.

When things work well, she brings a sense of purpose to the team. When teams understand and believe in the vision and align with the purpose, it's a beautiful thing. And if your team understands the organization's goals and their departmental and individual goals, you'll be well on your way. They will know what they're trying to accomplish and why—and leaders can hold them accountable.

The need for an execution partner, this #2 role, is probably the biggest need and most vital unlocking move for most entrepreneurs. Get it right and you're conquering the world; get it wrong and you're simply back to the drawing board. But the role is so needed, and the reward is so great, that I advocate for it with most entrepreneurs. It's become quite the specialty for my HireBetter team. (I tell people that your #2 is our #1 most recruited role!)

No Walk in the Park

This all sounds great, right? Bring in a kickass COO, everyone will click, and everything will be sunshine and roses!

Unfortunately, it ain't that easy. There are a number of things that need to happen to enhance your chances of success. That's part of why this is a multi-part chapter! It's not as simple as going out and hiring an operations person. I believe you need a PARTNER. This isn't a traditional employer/employee relationship. It's deeper than that and requires more in order to be successful.

Success depends on a number of factors. Natalie needs the skills and experience to complement you and build a great team. She also needs to mesh with you. You'll be working closely together, after all. Consider what your company needs now and for the foreseeable future, since not every Natalie has the same skills. You also need to make sure YOU'RE ready. If not, the relationship will be DOA.

If things go well, you just might end up handing over the CEO reins altogether—like I did!

How do you know you need to bring in an execution partner? When your business starts to hit that proverbial wall and your heroic efforts no longer move the needle. Maybe your growth has stagnated, or your profitability is down, or you're having production or quality control issues. These are common themes we've seen over the years.

Are *You* Ready?

Not everyone's ready to cede control or willing to admit they're not the best person to do certain jobs. Some of us can't handle not being a workaholic or doing only the jobs we enjoy and are great at. If that's you, that's your prerogative—stop reading and maintain status quo.

If you're not sure whether you're ready, here are a few signs that maybe you SHOULD be ready:

- Your company's growth has stagnated or plateaued.
- Your company's not as profitable as it used to be or is well below industry standard.
- You're self-aware enough to acknowledge that you need help scaling the business.
- Your life mandates it. Maybe you're missing

out on your kids growing up or time with your spouse or you had a major health scare—or some other life event.

- Your board or investors are demanding a change.
- You're simply TIRED.

Be prepared. If you do this right, things will change. You can no longer have your hands in every aspect of the business. You've got to give up some control and reduce everyone's reliance on you. But your team won't like having someone between you and them. More importantly, if you're trying to scale your company, your operating partner will certainly do things differently than you did.

Ryan Wasn't Ready . . .

Ryan was a client and a classic example of a visionary founder. He was on board with everything we discussed about his Talent Plan and knew things had to change. He had outgrown several team members, and he desperately wanted someone to own the day-to-day of the business. But even after he brought on Nathan as his operating partner, he couldn't get out of his own way. He constantly meddled and undermined Nathan. Their relationship didn't last long, and we quickly parted ways with Ryan as a client when he refused to own any part in the demise of their relationship.

"Ryan" is important because he was the inspiration for an article I later wrote, "When You're the Problem," which became the epilogue for this book.[15] The concept of the entrepreneur being the problem was so well-received that it may be the topic of my next book!

Is Your Company Ready?

Most legacy teams like things the way they are. They've been with you for a long time and have invested lots of time, energy, and emotion in the business. Now they're not good enough anymore? I told you this is hard.

They probably won't like having someone coming in from the outside and doing things differently. The right operator will give them goals, metrics, and expectations—and will hold them accountable. Trust me, most people on your legacy team won't like being held accountable.

Now seems like the right time to mention one very important point. Not everyone on your team is going to make it as you evolve—and that's OK. As much as that sucks to hear, you've got to be prepared for this possibility. When I brought Cisco in, I told him, "No one on the team is untouchable. There are several people I want to give every chance to succeed, but there are no sacred cows." Because if I had untouchable employees, I would be destroying his ability to build a culture of accountability.

Her Company Wasn't Ready . . .

Carolyn's company was a rising star in the tech field but seemed to have plateaued. Many times she presented her challenges to her YPO forum, and they repeatedly encouraged her to bring in an operator. After pushing back for years, she finally pulled the trigger and brought in Nathaniel as president.

He soon realized that Carolyn had a sacred cow on her team, a longtime friend who worked with her for so long that she felt like Nathaniel's rules didn't apply to her. Nathaniel found himself managing around, and often cleaning up after, her. He discussed this with Carolyn many times, but she refused to listen and was unwilling to even have a conversation with her friend. She truly was untouchable.

Nathaniel tried to make it work for over a year, but ultimately realized things weren't going to change. The situation was untenable. He ended up leaving the company, and Carolyn found herself back on the proverbial couch, crying to anyone who would listen. She simply wasn't ready to make the changes necessary to professionalize the company and move it forward.

Preparing Your Team

Even though your team may be uncomfortable with the concept of a new boss or losing the direct line to you, I've seen success through a tried-and-true approach—authenticity. If you're open and honest about your own shortcomings as a leader, they'll better understand the need for change. If you have thick skin, consider having your team anonymously do the quadrant exercise about you. What do THEY think your strengths and weaknesses are as a leader?

For me, I found that the team members who wanted the company to be successful and wanted to grow professionally knew we needed help to drive the company forward. And those who wanted a lifestyle business, who didn't want to push themselves, who liked the status quo—they pushed back on anything that disrupted their lives and pushed them out of their comfort zone. They were the ones who ultimately didn't make it as we moved toward scale.

A Look in the Mirror

Background

For most of this book, I've shared stories from my experience with HireBetter and TCG + Tatum, as well as direct experience advising hundreds of entrepreneurial clients for more than twenty-five years—mostly other people's stories.

This next part is very personal to me—because it's my story. You're going to get a front-row seat to my own experiences with Next-Level Natalie, warts and all.

In 2001 I founded a professional service firm, The Controller Group. Along with my partners, Brett Lawson and Kathy Schrock, we grew it substantially and ultimately sold the company to Tatum in 2006. When I bought HireBetter in 2011, I assumed we'd simply cut and paste TCG to replicate our success. Boy, was I wrong—and humbled! It wasn't that easy. Sure, I was new to recruiting, but I was confident clients would flock to our fresh approach. Didn't everyone know the traditional recruiting model was broken? I figured our only challenge would be managing growth.

Sleepless Nights

We did grow—that was true—even as we reinvented ourselves and evolved our business model, our differentiators, and our brand. We worked our tails off and had all the operational challenges and late nights you'd expect to find in a startup. It wasn't supposed to be so hard this time around!

During those early years, and after numerous sleepless nights, I asked myself, "Why am I doing this? I don't need to do this!" But I rationalized my workaholism by telling myself that the world needed what HireBetter had to offer.

It was tough but fun. We grew tremendously—well north of 50 percent for a few years. But I didn't think we were growing fast enough. I made investments to "scale" the company. Unfortunately, my investments weren't effective. They were expensive and we were just pissing away cash.

Whenever we got busy, the team got overloaded. My managers would say, "Kurt, the team is strapped, we need more people." I'd respond flippantly, "Then go get more people—we're scaling the business!" But we weren't scaling, we were throwing bodies at problems. We not only didn't have the operational discipline or experience to build the systems needed to scale, but we also didn't have the team to effectively challenge me when I wanted to make bad bets. And in fairness to my team at the time, I usually didn't listen when they did voice those concerns to me.

In hindsight, it took heroic efforts to accomplish what

we did—keeping the wheels on the bus while maintaining some semblance of profitability and evolving the company.

Struggles with Execution

Four years in and things looked great—from the outside. In addition to the growth, we built a solid brand and were Platinum sponsors of the YPO Global Leadership Conference. But internally, we were struggling. We started losing money, had accountability issues, and quite simply, weren't getting things done. I was doing my part. In true Visionary fashion, I gave them a new set of priorities daily. Why couldn't they get them done? (Please note the heavy sarcasm in those previous sentences!)

With that much growth, you'd think we'd be highly profitable. Nope. I rationalized that, and my minimum wage salary (and my partner's) by saying, "We're building for the future. We'll make it up when we sell the business." However, while we were doing good work and building a solid brand, we weren't building a business anyone would want to buy. On top of that, my business credit card bills were stacking up and our line of credit "for a rainy day" was maxed out. It's no wonder my stress-levels were through the roof. Looking back, I see why I lost a few key employees those years.

"Operational excellence" was a term I threw around as something to attain. "This year, we're going to be operationally excellent," and the team would try their best. Unfortunately, I didn't have a plan and we didn't have the team to make it happen. And as I said before, it sure didn't help when I shifted their priorities and introduced new ideas on a daily basis.

It became obvious that most of my leadership team liked my inability to hold them accountable. I think this was a key reason they fought me about adding a COO to the team. They insisted they could get us there—and maybe they eventually could have. But I truly don't think they wanted an outsider holding them accountable and telling them what to do!

Things were broken, but I didn't know how to fix them. I finally accepted that it's OK to not have all the answers. It's OK to lean on a few confidants and admit everything isn't perfect. This was hard to do but so empowering. I needed help, and failure wasn't an option. If I have one endearing quality, it's that I simply don't quit!

I called in the cavalry, reaching out to Mike Aviles, my good friend, YPO forum mate, and operational guru. I asked him to assess my business and help me find a path forward. But I had to be willing to give him access to EVERYTHING, warts and all. He needed my permission to be honest, to tell me that my baby was ugly. Talk about a humbling experience!

This is probably one of the hardest things for an entrepreneur to do. I'm a long-time member of YPO, and I've been involved in Vistage, EOS, and other CEO networking groups. There's a lot of pressure to put on airs, act like things are perfect. "We're crushing it! Record year! Problems? Not me—never heard of 'em."

Entrepreneurs are prideful. We don't want to admit we're failing—especially in a peer-to-peer network with lots of successful peers! But I was in uncharted territory and needed a fresh perspective. I decided there was no shame in seeking help. It wasn't easy, but I'm glad I did!

After a few days, Mike made his assessment, which wasn't exactly a surprise, but still hard to hear. The conversation went something like this:

> "*Kurt, you've got a problem. People you believe are key, are actually part of the problem. You've got a solid foundation of individual contributors, a trusted brand, and people like and respect you. But your operating model is broken, and you're overstaffed. There's no organizational structure and no accountability within the team. You've built a lifestyle business for everyone on your team—but you.*"

Looking into that mirror SUCKED! It was hard to admit that things were so broken.

> **Perception:** "You've built a great brand and record revenue. Congratulations!"
> **Reality:** "You've built a lifestyle business for everyone on your team—but you."

I asked Mike for his advice. I told him, "Every option's on the table." We spent most of our time evaluating these three options:

1. Admit defeat and close up shop. Problem was, I'm not a quitter!

2. Sell the company for whatever we could get. But there wasn't much value to an outsider.
3. Do the hard work needed to fix it. I LOVE what I do when things are going well. Let's go!

I consulted with Mike, sought the advice of other mentors, and prayed about it. I eventually decided to go ALL IN—Option Three. This meant investing heavily in an operating partner: someone stronger than me to do the heavy lifting to run the business and manage the P&L. This would allow me to focus on the things I enjoy, like business development, strategic talent planning, and building the HireBetter culture.

We didn't have much cash in the business to invest, but I had access to capital. Was I willing to risk it? On one hand, I didn't think I could afford to hire a "true" operating partner, but I was afraid I couldn't afford NOT to. I needed to make a bold move.

You may have heard the analogy of burning your boats—about Alexander the Great on the shores of Persia. He was facing a huge army and was completely outnumbered. Failure wasn't an option. He told his troops to burn their boats. "Win or die!" I doubled down. By making this investment, I was burning my boats.

Catch the rest of my story, including challenges and successes, in chapter 12. In the meantime, check out Intermission IV for tips on how to identify, recruit, and onboard your own operating partner—as well as some right and wrong ways to build your relationship.

INTERMISSION IV

NEXT-LEVEL NATALIE—WHEN AND HOW

The wife of a client made a beeline for me at a YPO event a few years ago. She gave me a big hug and said, "Thank you for giving me my husband back. Stephen's having fun at work, and he's a joy to be around again. Thank you!" Damn! That makes everything worthwhile.

As you can tell, I'm passionate about the operating partner concept. I'm firmly convinced that a huge key to success for visionary founders and entrepreneurial companies is an operating partner who can execute your vision. Partner with someone who complements you, shares your values and your work ethic—then go kick some ass!

In chapter 11, we established that visionary founders are really good at certain things unique to them. We encouraged you to focus on what you're good at, what you're passionate about, and frankly, what no one else can do . . . and that's typically NOT running day-to-day operations.

We've determined that you need to find your own Next-Level Natalie. Now what? How can you identify, attract, and build a relationship with this person who's so important to your success? And how the hell are you going to afford her? The short answer is . . . well, there is no short answer. We'll spend this chapter discussing these topics and more.

Looking ahead, in chapter 12, we'll discuss next steps now that Natalie's on board. We'll help you make the most of your unlocking move. And I'll keep it real, sharing more personal stories about my own operating partner journey. I'll include some challenges we had along the way and why its proven to be well worth it in the end.

How Do You Afford Next-Level Natalie?

Before we spend too much time talking about "finding" the right person, let's talk about how you're going to pay for her. Natalie ain't cheap. But mark my words, the right person is worth every penny. Where do you think Steve Jobs would be without Steve Wozniak, or Bill Gates without Paul Allen, or Sonny without Cher? I can assure you that those operating partners paid for themselves many times over. The reality is that you're not going to attract a world-class, next-level partner if you're offering mid-level compensation. It's just not happening!

But Kurt . . . we're struggling financially. How the hell can I afford such an expensive hire?

I get that question a LOT from entrepreneurs. I've also heard "you're crazy" and a few expletives thrown in more times than I can count.

I've actually been in your shoes and asked that question myself. When your back's against the wall and you're feeling overwhelmed, how on earth can you justify what it takes to attract and incentivize the right person? What I learned myself, and have seen repeatedly with clients, is that you really can't afford NOT to hire an operating partner. A good one is well worth the price tag!

That sounds great, but how do I make that happen?

The short answer: I'm confident that if you don't currently have an operating partner, your company is probably wasting a ton of money. You might be overstaffed, or inefficient, or spending unnecessarily, or simply not charging enough. In my case, it was all of the above!

Your operating partner will uncover enough low hanging fruit in her first six months to pay her annual salary. I AM 1,000 PERCENT CONFIDENT IN THAT STATEMENT. A good operating partner will implement systems, processes, and structure to stop the bleeding and pay for themselves. One recent client, a $5 million revenue company, hired their Natalie, who identified over $700,000 in unnecessary expenses in her first year. This alone paid her $200,000 salary—and then some! Not to mention the longer-term opportunities for improvement she identified.

Time and time again, I've had clients and friends who initially asked, "How can I afford to make this hire?" come back a year later and say something like, "Thank you! I shudder to think where I'd be if I hadn't hired her." It's truly remarkable to see the changes and cost savings that occur when a strong operator installs processes, oversight, and accountability into an entrepreneurial business.

How should I structure their compensation?

I tell clients they have three levers to pull in building compensation packages: base comp, bonus comp (short-term incentives), and equity (long-term incentives). For candidates who want more guaranteed base comp, offer them less equity upside, and vice versa. I've seen packages structured in hundreds of ways, and there's no wrong answer. Just don't skimp on compensation, and make sure you enroll them in the process of defining incentives. Their incentives should align with your goals as a company and yours as a significant shareholder.

When their compensation is heavily incentive-based, I encourage you to include some checks and balances to ensure their incentives aren't solely short-term focused. I say this because I've seen at least one operator whose incentives were based entirely on profitability, which made sense at the time. But she wasn't interested in investing in the future, since any investment in future growth meant lower short-term profits—which reduced her near-term bonus potential.

How to Find Next-Level Natalie

First things first

Before you go charging off looking for an operating partner, let's spend some time assessing what you need. We want to make sure we build your house with the right set of blueprints. Meaning, let's make sure you're looking for the right person with the right skills and experience to complement you and that their values align with yours.

Consider what your company needs right now. Some operators are growth-minded, some bring operational excellence, while still others are turnaround specialists who increase profitability by slashing costs. Some are roll-up-your-sleeves, lead-from-the-trenches leaders, while others are excellent managers but won't get their hands dirty. The leader you need depends on your business, where you are in the growth cycle, and the culture you're building.

You need a partner who complements you.

Most importantly, your new operating partner needs to mesh well with you. Some personalities just don't work well together, and that's OK. You're looking for culture fit as much as you're looking for background and experience. You're basically going to be professionally married to this person for a while, so take this process seriously!

Next, let's talk about what you want YOUR role to be. Think back on that quadrant exercise from chapter 11 where we mapped out your highest and best use, as well as the things you're bad at and hate doing. One of your goals should be finding a partner who does those things well. Turn your personal weaknesses into organizational strengths.

Most entrepreneurial companies need structure as leaders attempt to professionalize the organization. You need someone who can distill your vision into an actionable strategy. Then turn that strategy into an executable plan, complete with measurable outcomes and accountability. You need a partner who is a strong manager and coach, who can build and develop the team to take the company to the next level.

I think I've got that person on my team right now . . . a real up-and-comer.

I know leaders who have had success looking inside their organization for their operating partner. But many have failed trying. My main caution is to make sure the person you promote has your respect and that of the organization. It takes a special person and relationship to make it work. If they don't have your respect or if they're unable or unwilling to stand up to you, then you don't have a partner, you have an employee.

Many years ago, I had a junior partner who did a fantastic job at many things. She questioned a number of my decisions and often challenged me. But she didn't stand her ground when I pushed back. And she agreed with me way more than she should have. In fairness, this was before I became self-aware and before I learned of the Visionary/Integrator relationship, so things might have been different if we had a re-do. But mistakes like these are often how we learn.

The Search Process

Because I run HireBetter, an executive search firm specializing in high-growth, entrepreneurial companies, you'd think I'd recommend engaging a recruiter. Not necessarily. If you have the time, energy, and patience to devote to the process and you have strong recruiting and interviewing skills, then you should own the process. What I do recommend is running a full and exhaustive search. Don't hire the first person your banker, lawyer, or YPO buddy recommends. And don't settle. This position is too important to cut corners!

I've got an HR team;
I'll have them run this search.

Not so fast. In my experience, most in-house recruiters and HR departments simply aren't wired to understand the depth of this role and what's truly needed. They also don't typically do many searches of this magnitude. There are exceptions, but I usually see the best results when this hire and this search is owned by the entrepreneur—although you'll need help.

As I've mentioned in previous chapters, I encourage you to seek out an advisor or CEO peer: someone you know and trust. Ask them to be part of the process, serving as a sounding board and participating in interviews. They'll see things you don't. And if you're anything like me, they'll be better interviewers than you! Be patient. This isn't a traditional hire, so don't interview like it is.

The Interview Process

This process doesn't end once you've identified prospective candidates. This is a BIG deal! You're not culling through job boards or hiring the opportunistic friend of a friend we met in Pipeline Paul. In all likelihood, you're wooing a kickass leader away from another company. That's no simple task! You've got to do more than your standard interview to ensure you've found "the one." And don't forget, your prospective partner will be interviewing you as well, assessing you and your opportunity every step of the way.

This sounds like a lot of work.

It is . . . as it should be. There's nothing more important than getting this right. Your standard interview process simply won't cut it. You didn't get engaged after your first date with your future spouse, did you? At the risk of sounding overly dramatic, this is almost as important as selecting a spouse. I encourage you to spend quality time with your prospective partner. Meet in the conference room to whiteboard ideas. Get her perspective on your company and the role. Get to know her as a human being. Invite her and her spouse to dinner. It's OK to talk shop, but it's also OK to simply get to know each other. At HireBetter, Cisco was sold on the opportunity pretty quickly, but I think his wife had some reservations. I think our get-to-know-you dinner helped me win her over!

Wine and dine? I can do that!

It goes beyond just getting to know them, though. You want to see how they operate, how their mind works. As I outlined in Intermission I, give your finalists a case study. Present them with a challenge you're facing. Give them a week and access to your team—maybe even access to your systems and records. Have them present their plan to you and your board or leadership team. How'd they do? Did they present amazing work or simply mail it in? This also gives you a chance to see how they work with your team.

I'm going to include my team in this—they know what we need.

I understand why you might think it's a good idea to have your team "interview" your candidates. They know you well and they're going to work with this person, right? Not so fast. Look, your team's not going to like the idea of "structure" and "accountability," as we've discussed. In my case, most of them had grown accustomed to Kurt's style (and my inability to hold people accountable). It's impossible to interview your potential boss and be impartial. Do you honestly think a candidate who'll bring accountability and structure (and change) will be accepted by most of your legacy employees? NO! Many of them will look for the easiest target so they can maintain the status quo.

This is a tough decision to make on your own, but it's absolutely not a decision you make by consensus. I do believe it's OK for your team to meet your finalists. However, do it over drinks or a meal, not in a formal interview setting. Your team may get protective when they feel threatened. I've seen more than one prospective partner run off by the legacy team's hostility in an interview. You want the best candidate for the business—not necessarily the best candidate for your team's psyche!

It's a Balancing Act

Finally, please recognize there's a balance as you interview candidates and sell them your vision. For example:

- You want candidates to see the opportunity you have as a company, but you also want them to know about the challenges you face.
- You want to screen and vet them for their capabilities, but you also need to sell them on the opportunity and the impact they can make.
- You want them to see your flaws (so they're not surprised later), while also selling them some sizzle!
- The right candidates will be interviewing you as much as you're interviewing them. If they're not selective or asking loads of questions, they're probably not right for the role.

Relationship Building

Once you've identified, vetted, and engaged with a prospective operating partner, the hard part begins. You need to continue building a relationship, working toward a true partnership. Take this part seriously. There are many potential roadblocks that can derail your partnership and prevent this from working. You're not just co-workers, and you're not just CEO and employee—you're partners who are equally important to the health and success of the business.

Partners. Relationships. Success.
This really is like dating!

Yes! And the keys to a successful partnership are the same as most other relationships—trust, respect, and communication. Building your relationship on a foundation of trust requires a lot of work, and it's a two-way street.

It's critical that you're aligned on vision and expectations. What's your vision for the business and your respective roles? What are your expectations on growth and profitability, and your expectation for the timing of a potential exit? Make sure you don't set your future partner up for failure by communicating false expectations. For example, if you don't plan to step down in three years, don't tell them that you do! Be honest, even if you don't know the answer.

This will be hard work. Some candidates won't be up for that. We want a partner who is experienced, yet hungry—a leader looking for the challenge of building and scaling a successful business. We don't want Resume Ralph who's looking for a 9-to-5 job with health benefits and freedom to travel. We want a PARTNER for you.

Onboarding

How do I build that trust and
ensure we're aligned?

Spoiler alert: it already started. All that time you spent getting to know each other during the interview process was laying the foundation. The discussions you're having, the way you show up, the way you interact with each other, the subtle jokes you make to each other—they're all setting the stage for your working relationship. So, treat it that way.

The best way to ensure alignment is to begin the partnership on the same page. Again, no false expectations or unspoken hopes or dreams. Lay it all out on the front end. Then communicate regularly and often. Agree on the length of the onboarding period and what you'd like them to accomplish. We encourage allocating a full ninety days to allow your partner to get up to speed. I know that seems like a lifetime for most entrepreneurs, but they need enough time to ask questions, get to know the team, and understand the inner workings of the business and their role. This'll also give them a chance to build rapport with you and the team before they start making changes.

Too many times I've seen new leaders come in, guns blazing. They feel like they need to prove themselves to you or the team they've been brought in to lead. It rarely goes well. Imagine someone coming into your family and immediately telling you you're doing everything wrong. You wouldn't like it. At least get to know me before you tell me my baby's ugly!

OK, fair enough. But what should they be doing in those ninety days?

There are numerous resources out there to aid in the onboarding of new leaders. HireBetter launched an onboarding program a few years ago, and we're fans of Michael Watkins's bestseller *The First 90 Days: Proven Strategies for Getting Up to Speed Faster and Smarter.*[16] Here are a few top tips we've aggregated over the years:

1. **Accelerate her learning.** Give her access to everything, including your mind and her new team—any info that'll help her get up to speed and eventually run the company.
2. **Get alignment.** Maintain alignment with you but also identify potential misalignments within the team and develop initial plans to address them. But do not rush into action!
3. **Achieve early wins.** Perhaps these can come from your list of key initiatives or from conversations with the team. What are their struggles? Finding early wins will set the stage for a strong future relationship.
4. **Set realistic expectations.** Most visionary entrepreneurs want results yesterday. I'm no different. However, you need to let your operating partner get up to speed before making wholesale changes.
5. **Build the team.** A strong team is vital to your operating partner's success. Whether she's inheriting a team or building a new one, she must be able to assess, align, and mobilize every member of her team.

Don't expect things to magically change overnight. Stick to the ninety-day checkpoint and take it seriously. Recognize there will be turbulent waters ahead. Natalie will be doing things differently than you and will be holding people accountable. It's very likely that some members of your team won't make it as Natalie gets up to speed and starts making changes.

Check out chapter 12 for more tips on transitioning leadership to Natalie and building a strong working relationship with her, as well as the continuation of my personal journey with my own operating partners.

12

NEXT-LEVEL NATALIE (PART 2)

WORKING TOGETHER

"Hiring your #2 can be challenging. I've seen both good and bad examples over the years across over 875 clients at CEO Coaching International. However, I've consistently seen that if you're mutually aligned on goals, you have a great plan, a solid accountability system—and a world-class coach—you're well on your way to a strong partnership."

– **Mark Moses,** CEO and Founding Partner of CEO Coaching International and Author of *Make BIG Happen* and *Making BIG Happen*

Now that I've covered why you need Natalie and how to find, interview, and onboard her, what now? Everything's gonna be peaches and cream, right? C'mon! You know it's not going to be that easy! By definition, she'll do things differently than you. You're going to feel like your baby's being taken away. Not only that, but a number of your legacy employees will complain about some of the "rules" and "processes" she's implementing. I told you it wouldn't be easy!

It's hard work to build the relationship you need with Natalie—and the trust you'll need to develop in order for you to let go of parts of the business. In fact, it's going to feel unnatural or even scary at times. But when you've found the right partner and you're working well together, letting go will free you up to do what you're passionate about and what you're great at.

In this chapter I'll help you avoid some common pitfalls and learn to work together as equals. My prayer for you is a vision for what could be. Embrace this move for what it is: a move to unlock your company's potential—to unlock YOUR potential!

Working Together

This is hard stuff—going from being the go-to guy to having someone else running the day-to-day and professionalizing your organization. You're going to feel the need to involve yourself in a lot of things (some might call it meddling). And Natalie's going to have to find ways to keep you in the loop and involve you enough that you don't feel "put out to pasture."

The onus is on your new operating partner to keep you up to speed, but as the entrepreneur, you play a large role in their success (or failure). As you've heard me say before, it mostly comes down to trust, respect, and communication. Here are a few key things to consider as you embark on your relationship with your operating partner:

1. **Trust.** You must build your relationship

on a foundation of trust. There will be times when you'll question Natalie. Legacy employees will come to you with problems and complain about her and the way she does things. You can listen and coach, but you can't make decisions. If you make decisions, you'll be severely hampering Natalie's ability to do her job. After you hear them out, ask them how they would like to communicate the conversation to Natalie; this will demonstrate your support for her.

2. **Respect.** If you don't mutually respect one other, end the relationship now. Respect is required for success. Although the entrepreneur owns more equity in the business, you must treat each other as equals for this to work. And negative comments about each other to anyone in the company is a huge no-no.
3. **Communication.** You must communicate with each other early and often and present a united front to the team, or they'll be confused. I'm a huge fan of weekly meetings to hash things out and ensure you're aligned. Talk through opportunities, discuss challenges, and don't end the meeting until you're 100 percent in agreement with each other.
4. **Your operating partner is the boss when working "in" the business.**

> Your leadership team must be empowered to make decisions. Everyone is heard, including you, but Natalie is the final arbiter. This will be uncomfortable for you but is required to scale the business. As such, you're expected to present a united front to others and pull your weight. This helps avoid confusion with the team.

Things Not to Do as You Transition

Let's talk about a few things NOT to do. I've seen a few common (and critical) mistakes entrepreneurs make that we need to address. Both examples happen during the transition or onboarding period and deal with how the entrepreneur approaches sharing responsibilities early on. Sometimes, the entrepreneur passes off responsibility immediately and focuses on who-knows-what (maybe their golf swing?), and others don't hand off any authority to their operating partner.

Letting Go Too Soon

When you relinquish everything too soon, a few things happen. First of all, Natalie hasn't had time to learn the business, engage the team, and understand the opportunities or challenges that need to be addressed. She needs to learn the lay of the land, the systems in place, your industry, and the team, in order to implement changes to improve the business.

The second thing that happens when you immediately

hand things off is that your company suffers without you. Whether you like business development or not, if you've been the rainmaker since day one, the team will suffer if you go cold turkey. Eventually, you can stop doing the things you don't like, but for now, you need to allow time for the team to get there.

The third thing that happens when entrepreneurs let go too soon is more emotional—more personal. They can feel like they've lost their identity, like they're no longer needed. This is why it's so important for the operating partner to involve them as much or as little as they want, always communicating and staying on the same page. The entrepreneur still has a lot to give. Don't waste their gifts.

Holding on Too Tight

On the other hand, a lot can go wrong if you hold the reins too tight. Once Natalie is up to speed, she'll suggest some changes. Some will be small, but others will be more significant, like implementing technologies, processes, and structure to drive efficiencies and accountabilities. You'll be uncomfortable and your team will be uncomfortable. Change does that to people. And for you personally, you may feel some sense of "founder remorse." It's normal and understandable. Give yourself six to twelve months before you start to panic!

Your team may question Natalie's approach and may come to you, expecting you to have their backs. "This isn't how we've always done it. Are you sure this is what you want your company to become? I can't believe she's making me do [fill in the blank]."

Be careful. If you allow your team to keep coming to you after you've handed responsibilities to Natalie, you're effectively undermining her position and authority. You simply can't do that and have a successful relationship. Meddling is not an option. As we said before, you can listen and coach, but you can't make decisions.

Make no mistake. As we pointed out in Intermission IV, for Next-Level Natalie, there may be times that your operating partner doesn't work out, for whatever reason. There's a greater than zero chance that the blame for her not working out can be pinned on you—and you'll have to learn from that experience for next time. But there'll be other times when you'll simply have to terminate your operating partner.

Nothing Lasts Forever

There's a chance that an operating partner was great for one phase of your company's lifecycle and not-so-great for the next. You may have to part ways at some point. That's OK; it happened at my own company. There are very few silver bullets who are a perfect fit for every stage of your company's lifecycle.

In my case, Natalie was fantastic for what we needed at the time—cost containment and operational efficiencies. We went from losing money hand-over-fist one year to making a significant amount the next. But when it was time to grow again, she wasn't well-suited to be a growth leader. So we mutually parted ways, and I wouldn't change a thing. We were much better for having had her lead the team for eighteen months than we would've been without her.

It May Not Work the First Time

This isn't easy. We're dealing with human beings, and you're trying to work with someone who's basically your opposite in so many ways. There's a decent chance this won't work the first time. And if it doesn't, we strongly encourage you to try again. The benefits far outweigh the risks. Just make sure you learn lessons about yourself, the role, and your company so you can improve your chances of success next time.

Unrealistic Expectations

We've got a strategic partner who's going through this as I write this book. My friend Lawrence, the visionary entrepreneur, hired Nate as his operating partner in late 2020. Now they're parting ways nine months later. Lawrence told me Nate wasn't a good fit. He said he never should have hired an employee who doesn't sell or deliver services.

Huh? "Why do you want Nate to sell or deliver services—isn't that what your team does? Isn't that what YOU love to do?" I asked. This happens a lot. The entrepreneur is so myopic that he doesn't see the advantages of having Nate focus on running the business and building a strong team; he only sees that Nate's not producing revenue. I wanted to thump Lawrence on the head and remind him that he doesn't need another leader who does what he does! He needs someone to complement his skill set and build the organization for scale.

If you're self-aware, you'll learn a lot about yourself in the process and come out stronger in the end.

Unlocking Move

Bringing in the right operational partner can truly be an unlocking move—for you professionally and personally, and for the business as a whole. When you're doing what you're passionate about and great at—while working with a partner who complements you and is great at the things you suck at—it's liberating. I know it's hard to believe, but some people were born operators, and they love it!

Not only are you freeing yourself up, you're replacing yourself in certain areas with someone stronger than you. Maybe you're a bad manager, like me. Or maybe you're a relationship guy who sucks at building sales processes. Or you're an engineer who loves tinkering with new ideas but doesn't want to be the face of the company anymore. The point is, there are people out there who complement your skills and can free you up to follow your passion!

The best part that I probably don't focus on enough is this: with the right operating partner, your company will be more profitable—much more. Talk about a win-win-win!

Real World 1.0

Remember how I told you this whole operating partner thing might not work out the first time? Some might say my first attempt didn't work out at HireBetter. But I'd argue that she was exactly what we needed at the time. And I have no regrets.

In the previous chapter, I shared with you some stark news about HireBetter back in 2014. We were bleeding cash, my team was bloated, and my good friend Mike didn't pull any punches when he told me, "You've built a lifestyle business for everyone on your team—but you."

In late 2015 we brought on Natalia as my first operating partner, and she delivered exactly what we needed at the time. It was critical that we prove we could make money, so we charged her with improving net income. We also asked her to remove unnecessary costs and fix inefficient processes. You might call it a restructuring or even a turnaround—but Natalia was the right person for the job.

Once she was onboarded and had fully assessed our situation, she focused on a few key areas: the team, topline revenue, and inefficient spending. She successfully raised our prices and improved our contracting process. She removed a lot of fat from the team, reducing headcount by about 36 percent. She also identified some silly non-payroll spending. For example: weirdly we had thirty-five VOIP phone licenses, but only needed sixteen; we had two 800 numbers when we needed zero; and we had twenty LinkedIn Recruiter licenses but needed only eight. Thousands of dollars wasted! These are just a few of the dumb ways we wasted money.

Natalia was exactly what the doctor ordered—at first. Unfortunately, once we got through the initial slash-and-burn and decided it was time to grow again, it was a different story.

Natalia's expertise was cutting costs. She wasn't comfortable with risk or investing in growth. And she was bonused on net income. So, when I determined we needed a sales leader to build a scalable sales engine and augment my feast-or-famine BizDev efforts, she balked. Was this because a sales leader's compensation would reduce her bonus in the short term? I'm not sure, but I knew we needed to invest in a sales leader to get where we wanted to go.

In hindsight, I realized she simply wasn't built for growth. You could argue Natalia wasn't a true operating partner, she was more of a restructuring specialist. Could I have engaged her, or a project-based consultant, to do what she did? Possibly. But at the end of the day, I'm very grateful for Natalia. HireBetter got the result we needed in our eighteen months together, I learned a lot about myself and my team, and she moved on to bigger and better things.

Note to self for next time: when setting up bonus structures for your operating partner, make sure you include both short-term and long-term bonus incentives as well as counter measures, so Natalie keeps the big picture in perspective.

Real World 2.0

When it came time to grow and scale the company, we needed a different mindset than Natalia. I went large and convinced a YPO friend of mine to join the team. Nate had just come off of a successful exit as an operator and wanted to do it again.

For the next year we focused on investing in the future and growing HireBetter to be THE strategic talent partner for entrepreneurial companies. Nate was solid and a calming influence for the team. Unfortunately, his time was cut short at HireBetter when he had a health scare about twelve months in. We mutually decided he needed to focus on his health.

Nate's now in a great spot, health wise, and HireBetter's doing great. Cisco Sacasa joined us as our president in late 2019 and has been kicking ass ever since; so much so that I promoted him to CEO shortly thereafter. That wasn't a misprint. I knew Cisco would be a better CEO than me, and I wanted to be unshackled from the day-to-day and all that the CEO title entails. I wanted to focus on the things that fuel me. I sure didn't need the CEO title to feed my ego.

Letting Go

I gotta be honest, there were times I struggled to "let go"—and still do from time to time. It made me realize how hard this is for our clients. How does a founder let go of everything they've built and let other people run it? Emotionally, it felt like handing my eighteen-year-old the car keys and watching him drive off to college. I knew I'd given him the tools to succeed, but there's still part of me that wants to keep a close eye on him!

Obviously, Cisco and my team aren't leaving home for the first time. He's a proven leader with experience leading growth companies like ours. We knew each other for several years prior and respected each other. And we've been working hard to foster the partnership we know we need to build HireBetter.

What a Year!

When Cisco was being onboarded, little did we know that COVID-19 would shut down the world before he hit the ninety-day mark! Let me say this unequivocally—without Cisco by my side in 2020, I'm not sure we would've made it. He has an ability to plan out contingencies, assess risks, and assess the cost of each option. I don't have that skill. I did play my part: rallying the team and our clients as we all strived to survive.

Cisco and I determined that survival was no longer the goal. We wanted to make key investments so we could thrive on the other side. So "Survival and Thrival" became our mantra at HireBetter and for the entrepreneurial community we serve.

Beyond the challenge that was 2020, Cisco successfully distilled my vision for HireBetter into an executable plan. Through a number of deep discussions, he helped me articulate where we wanted to be in five years. He then broke that down into a plan for the organization and for each department and team member. We now have yearly, quarterly, and monthly goals and objectives, and the team is held accountable. The team is on fire.

Free to Be Me!

The best part? I'm not in charge! I get to focus on what I'm great at! Cisco runs the company and ensures everything we do is based on our core values, our purpose, and our vision. We always THOUGHT we were purpose-driven (doesn't everyone?), but now we actually are! Everyone understands their role and expectations—and they're fired up to build a great company that lives up to our impact statement: *We impact lives by connecting and empowering good people to build great companies.*

When I gave up the CEO title, I received tons of inspiring comments from friends, colleagues, and LinkedIn connections. I told them I wasn't retiring—and I'm more fired up than ever. I like to think of it as "stepping aside," rather than stepping down. I'm getting out of the way and letting Cisco do his thing. But recently, a friend told me she loved how I "stepped up" by recognizing that I was previously holding my business back. I like that. However you define it, taking those steps are hard, but definitely worth it in the long run.

Moving Forward

In March 2021 I was sitting in a routine, monthly leadership meeting. Cisco was leading a discussion about goals for Q1. Where did we stand and what should Q2 goals look like? I felt a sense of calm and just sat back and relaxed, thinking to myself, *Damn, I'm SO unnecessary in this meeting!*

The team is a machine; they know what they need to do, and they're driving THEIR teams based on the plan. They have high expectations, they're engaged in the process, and they're growing personally and professionally. It's hard to describe how I felt in that moment. Kind of like a proud parent—but in a "this is f-ing cool" kind of way.

And remember how HireBetter was overly reliant on me and my network for new business? We've built a sales engine and new clients are coming in daily—I have no idea how they found us. Isn't that great? It sounds silly, but it's a REALLY good feeling. I'm officially no longer a "have to have" on the sales front, I'm a "nice to have." This allows me to turn my attention to the future. I can now spend time evangelizing our mission, seeking out M&A opportunities, and dreaming up new products and partnerships.

If my personal feelings can't sway you, maybe these numbers can: in the twelve months since Cisco took over as CEO, we survived COVID, invested in infrastructure to fuel future growth, increased revenue by 50 percent, grew profitability by 300 percent, and we're about to sign a letter of intent to make the first of many acquisitions. That's what you can get when you mitigate the entrepreneur's weaknesses and replace them with the strengths of a strong operating partner—and you work hard to develop and maintain trust, respect, and communication.

EPILOGUE

WHEN YOU'RE THE PROBLEM

*"I've made bad hires, and made poor decisions on promotions, and there's no question I've been guilty of letting others hang around way too long. I finally came to the realization that it's not them, it's me. I looked in the mirror and realized—**I'm the problem.**"*

– Undisclosed Entrepreneur in Texas

In this book, I've outlined a number of employee archetypes you'll likely come across on your entrepreneurial journey. I'm quite sure several of them are familiar to you. You may have a Bounce-Around Betty or Side-Hustle Sam on your team right now. You may have interviewed Resume Ralph or Pipeline Paul. Or maybe you've heard horror stories from peers about Techno Tim.

As your journey continues, you'll cross paths with other characters in this book. I hope the stories and advice I've laid out helps you avoid some of the lessons I've either learned the hard way or witnessed first-hand.

With the right tools, you can create a great culture to build a winning team, mitigate the risk of bad hires, and confidently handle inevitable issues with your team.

You know that growing companies need talent to win, but you also know it's not just about your team. There's one key element we haven't yet addressed: You could follow every bit of advice in this book and still end up bankrupting your company. In fact, you can hire expensive recruiters to find great talent, pay employees above-market comp, and offer the best perks in the world—but some of you will still figure out how to screw it all up.

To Put It Bluntly . . . Sometimes *You're* the Problem!

Entrepreneurs wear a lot of hats. You're hiring and managing employees, growing revenue, raising capital, negotiating M&A transactions, setting the vision, and developing new products. And that's just a regular Tuesday! Hell, some of you probably manage your own schedule and do your own books.

As we saw with legacy employees like Right-Hand Rita and Who's Your Mike, the entrepreneurial, can-do spirit is an absolute must in the early days. But at some point, it becomes, at best, unscalable—and at worst, downright destructive. This goes for you too.

The very qualities that made you successful as a founder—like being a big thinker with tons of ideas, your risk-taking attitude with minimal regard for what could go wrong, and your 24/7 work ethic—are actually HARMFUL as the company turns the corner. Constant shifting of priorities doesn't scale and can lead to burnout or loss of key employees.

This shifting of priorities is just one of the reasons that sometimes YOU'RE THE PROBLEM.

The Truth Hurts

A prospective client recently shared with me how he hired a seasoned consultant to "fix my operations." The company had been tremendously successful, but now orders were outpacing their ability to deliver. The duct-tape-and-binding-twine method was no longer working.

The situation went from bad to worse when one of his major customers conducted a facility audit—and they failed. Thus, the reason for bringing in the seasoned consultant, who spent thirty days observing, asking questions, pulling reports, and digging in. Among the findings of the consultant was this gem: "In order for the company to be successful, the CEO WILL NEED TO STEP DOWN AND BRING IN NEW LEADERSHIP." Ouch.

Based on my knowledge of the situation and discussions with the CEO, I agree that he did need to step down. He clearly played a role in the company's issues. The question was, would he continue to conduct "business as usual" or recognize that HE needed to evolve if he truly wanted to scale?

Luckily, he was humble enough to recognize that he didn't know everything—there was some truth to the statement. In reality, the company had outgrown him in several key ways. While he still had a knack for product development and customer relationships, he lacked the operational skills and managerial capabilities to scale the business and achieve his long-term growth goals. Deep down inside he knew HE was the biggest reason why the company's operations were so chaotic.

Changing the Plan

As we learned with Next-Level Natalie, there's a right way and a wrong way to handle change. Most entrepreneurs are go-getters, quick-thinkers, and problem-solvers, and they expect things to happen at the frenetic pace they're used to. But when a new leader arrives to professionalize operations, change can't happen too quickly. The new leader needs time to get to know the company, meet with customers, and learn the product. Most of us know that, but when push comes to shove, can you honestly stop yourself from meddling or getting upset when things don't happen fast enough?

One particularly interesting example was a first-time entrepreneur I worked with a few years ago. She knew she needed help to scale her business—an operating partner to build the infrastructure required to make her vision a reality. When she hired Nathan, she had a pretty good idea of what she expected from him. We worked with her to map out what a successful first ninety days would look like and a vision for their working relationship.

According to the plan, Nathan's first thirty days were specifically set up for him to get to know the situation, as I described above. I knew something was amiss on day five when she called me complaining that it had been a week and he hadn't chosen a new accounting system yet!

The following week, she informed Nathan that the company had a huge marketing opportunity. The "opportunity" was to spend the equivalent of two months' revenue on a campaign, and she needed Nate to plan and execute it. Mind you, this was day ten, and the company already had problems fulfilling orders! To make a long story short, the entrepreneur was the problem, and she couldn't get out of her own way. Even with clear expectations set at the beginning, she wanted to continue her "ready-fire-aim" ways, hamstringing her new partner before he even had a chance.

Unspoken Expectations

By now you know that when you onboard a new employee, it's important to set expectations early, and gain alignment. With regular one-on-one communication to discuss status, changes, and surprises, you should remain aligned. Priorities will naturally shift, especially in entrepreneurial companies, but if you communicate regularly, at least you'll be on the same page.

But when you DON'T communicate effectively, even trivial things can cause major problems. One of my favorite examples comes from a founder who had a thing against special treatment. One of the ways this manifested was in his disdain for "reserved parking" for company executives, for which there were five spaces in the company parking lot.

The founder believed it sent a bad message to the team if he used his spot—like he was superior to the other 180 employees. So each morning, he parked as far away from the door as possible. Then, when his new CFO started and parked in one of the handy-dandy reserved spots every morning, it drove the founder batshit crazy! Of course, he'd never mentioned this unwritten rule to his CFO and also never mentioned that it bothered him. In the founder's head, the CFO was blatantly screaming, "I'm better than everyone else!" That wasn't the only reason the two ultimately parted ways within the first year, but it was one of the straws that broke the camel's back.

Shifting Priorities

As entrepreneurs, you know we want things to move uber-fast. We have a hundred ideas a week and want to put them into action. Then we get frustrated with our team's "inability to execute" when our list of unfinished projects grows longer. We compound this frustration by giving our poor team new priorities the following week, and the next.

We crave the stability, systems, and structure that an operating partner is supposed to bring, but we lose patience with the very methodical pace that ensures their success. While this sounds crazy to an outsider, it's hard to see within ourselves. We simply don't realize the impact our scattered approach has on our teams.

Two Is Better Than One

After I launched The Controller Group, I was fortunate to have been introduced to Brett Lawson very early on. He ended up being my business partner and saved my ass as my operating partner. Brett and I had very different perspectives. In fact, we were different in a number of ways.

He was direct, analytical, and a pain in the ass—and we disagreed a lot. But I respected the hell out of him, and he respected me. He knew my harebrained ideas had some semblance of credibility, and I knew his execution strategies were sound. We co-developed solutions. Sometimes the answer was mine, sometimes his, but most often, it was something in between.

We balanced each other out. Individually, both of us could have been the problem! But because we brought our unique strengths, we trusted and respected each other, and we communicated well enough to arrive at the right answer. We were tremendously successful; I couldn't have built TCG without Brett, and he would tell you that he couldn't have built it without me.

What's Next?

When I first set out to write this book, it was going to be all-encompassing. Part of it was going to be about the employees I've met during my almost thirty years working with entrepreneurs. And part of it was going to be about some of the pain-in-the-ass entrepreneurs I've encountered along the way. In the end, the right answer was to focus on the team in this book and share *When You're the Problem* (working title) down the road, in the next book.

In my case, I KNEW I was part of the problem. In fact, in 2020 I decided to step down as CEO of HireBetter and take on a new role as chief evangelist. (We don't have a board, so chairman of the board sounded hollow.) It wasn't necessarily that I was a bad CEO, but I recognized that the visionary role I played in my company clashed with its day-to-day needs. I was holding us back.

Candidly, the CEO role was holding me back too! In my new role, I've been able to focus on what I do best, which includes HireBetter vision and strategy, key relationships, and Strategic Talent Planning with clients—as well as things like writing this book, speaking at conferences and events, and conducting CEO forums. And Cisco's appreciative that I've gotten the hell out of his way so he can do his thing.

I'll finish where I began—I hate most business books. This was never meant to be a top-down edict, but rather the start of a conversation. I welcome your thoughts on this book and each of its characters. Let me know what you think. And I invite you to share additional characters I may have missed—ones you've seen in your career, whether you're the entrepreneur or part of an entrepreneurial team. Join me at www.WhosYourMike.com.

APPENDIX

CUTTING ROOM FLOOR

I hope you've enjoyed *Who's Your Mike?* and you've been able to glean a few tips and strategies for dealing with characters like these in your own company. If you're like all of the entrepreneurs I shared earlier drafts of this manuscript with, you recognize a bunch of these characters from your own entrepreneurial journey.

It isn't lost on me that I couldn't possibly cover EVERY single character in a single book. In fact, I've got a notebook full of other ones I've seen—from jackasses to superheroes, and everyone in between! Some of the characters who follow are just half-baked concepts that ended up getting wrapped into other chapters in the book, some are truly unique but probably didn't deserve their own chapter, and some could very well form the basis of another book!

As you read this book, I'm confident many of you were thinking something like: "Where's the girl who never turns her Zoom camera on and is always on mute?" or "What about the tightwad accountant?" or "Where's the dude who always seems to be distracted by a personal problem?"

If you've been thinking something like that, then this is your chapter! Think of it as a collection of characters who didn't quite make the cut: little vignettes, outtakes even. Some stories don't need their own chapter.

Tightwad Tommy

Tommy's a classic accountant who thinks he's managing his own personal checkbook every time the company spends a dime. You've heard the adage, "You've got to spend money to make money." Tommy disagrees wholeheartedly and thinks it's the stupidest thing he's ever heard! There's no way he should work with an entrepreneur. He simply doesn't get it, and you butt heads at every turn. He gets frustrated when you take your million-dollar client to a fancy dinner, he wants only off-brand Keurig pods, and he asks people to limit their paper towel usage to one sheet at a time.

While I appreciate Tommy conserving cash as if it were his own—we're a growing company, and we definitely can't penny pinch our way to the next level!

Big-Spender Bertha

Bertha is the exact opposite of Tommy. She's your VP of Sales and seems like she's incapable of NOT spending money! And if you have a Tommy paired with a Bertha, bring some popcorn, 'cuz there's gonna be a show. I happened to work with a Bertha early on in my career when I was the controller for a startup (maybe I was the tightwad?). Here I was, trying to extend our runway and count f-ing pens—while Bertha spent money like a drunken sailor! It didn't help that I thought she was a blowhard who couldn't close a sale to save her life!

Paycheck Pete

In entrepreneurial companies, your team's got to be willing to roll up their sleeves and bust their hump to grow the company. We all know folks like Paycheck Pete, who somehow fell through the cracks. Pete probably came from a more corporate or even governmental background. He's used to clocking in at 8:30 and clocking out at 5:00 sharp—with a thirty-minute lunch and a few smoke breaks in between! No matter what fire you're fighting, Pete's done and out the door at 5:00. Send him an email or text over the weekend? You won't get a response until Monday morning. Just make sure you're not late with his paycheck.

Personal-Problem Polly

Polly's a decent employee. Not an A-player by any stretch, but she's OK. The problem is . . . well, Polly's got a lot of problems—like, the worst-luck-in-the-world kind of problems. It may be little things, but they never seem to stop. It might be car issues, or her alarm clock doesn't go off. Then her uncle gets sick, or her parents split up. Then she needs dental implants or has complications from LASIK.

When you see her calling, you simply roll your eyes and wonder, *What now, Polly?*

You want to be compassionate, but you've got work to do! Your team's losing confidence in you because they think Polly's playing you like a fiddle.

Ghosting Ginny

This one's becoming more common in the post-pandemic world of remote work. Ginny actually does decent work—when you can reach her! But damn, she's hard to track down. In fact, you're pretty sure she's using Tim Ferriss's *The 4-Hour Workweek* as her playbook, because she seems to have mastered the "sense of selective ignorance" espoused by Ferriss. Where is she?!?! On the flip side, Ginny sure is charming and kisses your ass every chance she gets.[17]

I just don't trust folks like Ginny—not because I want to micromanage, but because I'm building a business and I need a team in the foxhole with me.

Firefighter Fran

In entrepreneurial companies like ours, there're a lot of fires to put out! You're scratching and clawing every day, and you rely on team members who can solve problems. This can be a great attribute to have in an employee, and Fran sure loves to be the hero. But beware of Fran! What you don't see is that a ton of the fires she put out were actually CAUSED by Fran! Maybe accidentally or perhaps purposefully—she stirs the pot, then swoops in to save the day.

This one is hard to see, but if you have a Fran, you'll soon appreciate the concept of addition by subtraction. Once she's gone, your team will share horror stories about Fran and her antics.

Friend of Founder (FOF)

We've discussed numerous times how founders usually hire whoever they can get in the early days—brothers, friends, neighbors, etc. And that's OK. Just make sure you hold those friends and relatives to the same standard as the rest of your team. As soon as you show favorable treatment to FOFs, you lose credibility with the rest of your team. By the same token, as you grow and recruit new talent, your team will likely cringe every time you suggest hiring another FOF.

Teflon Tony

Damn, he seems to be so much quicker pointing his finger than raising his hand. It's never his fault, and he always over promises. The vendor failed to deliver, the client is too picky, we don't charge enough, we charge too much, etc. They're all just well-documented excuses at this point.

Buddy the Backstabber

You like Buddy—he has his finger on the pulse of the office. You can count on him to share critical information about team morale and impending issues. He works hard to stay in your good graces—in fact, he's usually the first to ask for your input or compliment your leadership. Buddy is invaluable and you can't imagine losing him. What you don't know is that he's a backstabber. He makes himself look good at the expense of his co-workers. Dig a little deeper, and you may find that many team members you've lost over the years cite Buddy as the reason they left.

The Don

Don was initially your "silver bullet." You built a successful business, but after ten years you were tired. You met Don at church, he'd previously been a COO, and he sure seemed like a smart guy! You end up bringing him on. He convinced you to hand him the keys and now EVERYTHING runs through Don. No decision gets made without him. He's a control freak and he won't admit when he needs help. Did I mention Don's volatile personality and his tendency to blow up at people? Your "silver bullet" has quickly become your Achilles' heel!

Other Outtakes

- **Turnover Theresa** is a decent employee but jumps ship at the first offer that pays her a few dollars more. You're not Theresa's first.
- **Micro-Manager Molly** can't get out of her own way. She must have everything done her way.
- **Wanda the Worrier** is never willing to take a risk or accept your risk-taking. She's exhausting to entrepreneurs, because she's always looking at what can go wrong versus what can go right.
- **Napoleonic Nick** is a first-time manager who

beats the team up because he wants and demands their respect. He doesn't have the maturity to know that the team simply doesn't respect him.

- **Millennial Mark** thinks all business perspectives should go through the lenses of Millennials and Gen Z. He doesn't respect you because you "don't get it." He's hungry but not humble—with zero EQ to speak of.
- **Happy Holly** doesn't like conflict and doesn't like it if she has even an inkling that the team's not happy. Why can't we all get along?

Got more?

Do you have additional characters you've seen on your journey? Whether you have a good story or maybe even a character I should consider for a future article or future book, let me know who they are—the crazier the better! Share them with me at WhosYourMike.com.

ACKNOWLEDGMENTS

Over the past dozen or so years I've had numerous conversations with friends and clients about talent challenges in entrepreneurial companies. I won't be able to list all of the participants in those conversations but please know that they were powerful and set the stage for this book. People like Melinda Owens, Brett Lawson, Ron Kessler, Al Chase, Johnathan Hines, Jamie Wheal, Clint Greenleaf, John Weaver, Doug Tatum, Bob Litschi, John Flynn, Brian Utley, Rand Stagen, Rich Martin, Ryan Shultz, Matt Becker, Craig Wiley, Jonathan Ulrich, David Washburn, Mathias Ihlenfeld, Jacquie Hart, Tom West, Melanie Shaffer, Amy Ancira, Doug Cunningham, Abe Paul, Paul Hedrick, Scott Jensen, Suzi Sosa, Carl Natenstedt, Cisco Sacasa, Beth Goff-McMillan, Jack Nelson, Curtis Eggemeyer, Rick Lundbom, Matt Coscia, Abbie Martin, Chris Carmouche, and Johnnie Johnson. I'm sure I'm leaving out quite a few. But these conversations and interactions with dozens, if not hundreds of clients formed the foundation for this book. Thank you all for your candor and unique perspectives.

Carl, your encouragement on the Appalachian Trail

in 2020, and your willingness to brainstorm employee archetypes and stories for HOURS, was probably the turning point where the book went from cool concept to "I'm f-ing doing this." Thank you.

When I wrote the *Who's Your Mike?* blog article years ago, I had no idea how popular it would be amongst my peers and clients. Well, thanks to you, it's now not only the Introduction to this book, it started a tsunami of ideas about other characters you've met on your respective entrepreneurial journeys. To each of you who shared your stories with me—thank you. This book is for you, and I hope your story helps a new generation of entrepreneurs build successful companies that do great work.

I'd like to thank my devoted team of HireBetterans who gave me the opportunity to pull this off and who tirelessly serve our entrepreneurial clients. I know full well how much of a pain in the ass entrepreneurs can be to work with (myself included)—and I thank you for all the great work you do for them. Your work inspired this book and your words encouraged me to put myself out there!

Special thanks to the team who worked so diligently behind the scenes to make this dream a reality, including my friends at Content Capital and Zilker Media—and Sebastian Cudicio, our illustrious illustrator.

Last but certainly not least, I want to thank my nephew Evan Spencer and my friend Rod Kurtz, whose collaboration from beginning to end made this book possible. There is no chance this book happens without your dedication and commitment. Evan, you're a master at putting my "word vomit" into some semblance of structure and I appreciate all of the time you dedicated to this endeavor. And it was very cool to have the opportunity to get to know you so well during the process. Rod, you're a word master and your perspective on business and people made you a perfect partner in crime for this book. I now consider you a lifelong friend and I'm blessed to have had the opportunity to work with such a talented person.

REFERENCES

Books

Burlingham, Bo. Small Giants: *Companies That Choose to Be Great Instead of Big*. New York: Portfolio/Penguin, 2016.

Collins, James C. *Good to Great: Why Some Companies Make the Leap—and Others Don't.* New York: HarperCollins, 2001.

Commons, John R. *The Distribution of Wealth.* New York: Macmillan and Co., 1893.

Ferriss, Tim. *The 4-Hour Workweek: Escape 9-5, Live Anywhere, and Join the New Rich.* New York: Crown Publishers, 2007.

Harnish, Verne. *Mastering the Rockefeller Habits: What You Must Do to Increase the Value of Your Growing Firm.* New York: SelectBooks, 2002.

——. *Scaling Up: How a Few Companies Make It . . . and Why the Rest Don't.* San Francisco: Instaread, 2014.

Hesselbein, Frances and Paul M. Cohen, eds. *Leader to Leader: Enduring Insights on Leadership from the Drucker Foundation's Award-Winning Journal.* San Francisco: Jossey-Bass, 1999.

Lencioni, Patrick. *Overcoming the Five Dysfunctions of a Team: A Field Guide for Leaders, Managers and Facilitators.* San Francisco: Jossey – Bass, 2005.

Moses, Mark. *Make Big Happen: How to Live, Work, and Give Big, for CEOs, Entrepreneurs, and Leaders.* Charleston, SC: Forbes Books,

2016.

Patterson, Kerry, Joseph Grenny, Ron McMillan, and Al Switzler. *Crucial Conversations: Tools for Talking When Stakes Are High.* New York: McGraw Hill, 2002.

Pritchett, Bob. *Fire Someone Today: and Other Surprising Tactics for Making Your Business a Success.* Nashville: Thomas Nelson, 2006.

Sinek, Simon. *Start with Why: How Great Leaders Inspire Everyone to Take Action.* New York: Portfolio/Penguin, 2009.

Smart, Bradford D. *Topgrading: How Leading Companies Win by Hiring, Coaching, and Keeping the Best Players.* New York: Portfolio/Penguin, 2005.

Smart, Geoff and Randy Street. *Who: The A Method for Hiring.* Boston, MA: Tantor Media, Inc., 2008.

Tatum, Doug. *No Man's Land: Where Growing Companies Fail.* New York: Portfolio/Penguin, 2008.

Warrillow, John. *Built to Sell: Creating a Business That Can Thrive Without You.* New York: Portfolio/Penguin, 2011.

Watkins, Michael. *The First 90 Days: Proven Strategies for Getting up to Speed Faster and Smarter.* Boston: Harvard Business Review Press, 2013.

Wickman, Gino. *Traction: Get a Grip on Your Business.* Dallas: BenBella Books, 2011.

Wickman, Gino and Mark C. Winters. *Rocket Fuel: The One Essential Combination That Will Get You More of What You Want from Your Business.* Troy, MI: Business News Publishing, 2016.

Articles

Cappelli, Peter. "Why We Love to Hate HR . . . and What HR Can Do about It." *Harvard Business Review*, 6 July 2015, https://hbr.org/2015/07/why-we-love-to-hate-hr-and-what-hr-can-do-about-it.

Leonhardt, Megan. "Job-Hopping Heats Up: 65% of U.S. Workers Are Looking for a New Job." *Fortune.com*, 20 August 2021, https://fortune.com/2021/08/20/us-workers-looking-for-jobs/.

Ryan, Liz. "Ten Reasons Everybody Hates HR." *Forbes*, 28 July 2016, https://www.forbes.com/sites/lizryan/2016/07/27/ten-reasons-everybody-hates-hr/?sh=12677905af4a.

Wilkin, Kurt. "When You're the Problem." *KurtWilkin.com*, 1 December 2019, https://www.kurtwilkin.com/connections/2019/12/1/when-youre-the-problem.

Other

Fuqua, Antoine. *Training Day*. Burbank, CA: Warner Bros., 2001.

ENDNOTES

1. James C. Collins, *Good to Great: Why Some Companies Make the Leap—and Others Don't* (New York: HarperCollins, 2001), 41.; Verne Harnish, *Mastering the Rockefeller Habits: What You Must Do to Increase the Value of Your Growing Firm* (New York: SelectBooks, 2002), 17; Gino Wickman, *Traction: Get a Grip on Your Business* (Dallas: BenBella Books, 2011), 81.

2. Collins, *Good to Great*, 13.

3. *Training Day*, directed by Antoine Fuqua (Burbank, CA: Warner Bros, 2001).

4. From the best-selling book *Traction* by Gino Wickman and copyrighted by EOS Worldwide.

5. Collins, *Good to Great*, 42.

6. Bradford D. Smart, *Topgrading: How Leading Companies Win by Hiring, Coaching, and Keeping the Best People* (New York: Portfolio/Penguin, 2005), 7–8.

7. John R. Commons, *The Distribution of Wealth* (New York: Macmillan and Co., 1893).

8. Peter Cappelli, "Why We Love to Hate HR . . . and What HR Can Do about It," *Harvard Business Review*, 6 July 2015, https://hbr.org/2015/07/why-we-love-to-hate-hr-and-what-hr-can-do-about-it; Liz Ryan, "Ten Reasons Everybody Hates HR," *Forbes*, 28 July 2016, https://www.forbes.com/sites/lizryan/2016/07/27/ten-reasons-every-

body-hates-hr/?sh=12677905af4a.

9. Collins, *Good to Great*, 41.

10. Megan Leonhardt, "Job-Hopping Heats Up: 65% of U.S. Workers Are Looking for a New Job," Fortune.com, August 20, 2021, https://fortune.com/2021/08/20/us-workers-looking-for-jobs/.

11. Warren Bennis, "The Secrets of Great Groups," in *Leader to Leader: Enduring Insights on Leadership from the Drucker Foundation's Award-Winning Journal*, eds. Fraces Hesselbein and Paul M. Cohen (San Francisco: Jossey-Bass, 1999), 29–33.

12. Verne Harnish, *Scaling Up: How a Few Companies Make It . . . and Why the Rest Don't* (San Francisco: Instaread, 2014), 6.

13. Gino Wickman and Mark C. Winters, *Rocket Fuel: The One Essential Combination That Will Get You More of What You Want from Your Business* (Troy, MI: Business News Publishing, 2016).

14. Wickman and Winters, *Rocket Fuel* and Wickman, *Traction.*

15. Kurt Wilkin, "When You're the Problem," KurtWilkin.com, December 1, 2019, https://www.kurtwilkin.com/connections/2019/12/1/when-youre-the-problem.

16. Michael Watkins, *The First 90 Days: Proven Strategies for Getting Up to Speed Faster and Smarter* (Boston: Harvard Business Review Press, 2013).

17. Tim Ferriss, *The 4-Hour Workweek: Escape 9-5, Live Anywhere, and Join the New Rich* (New York: Crown Publishers, 2007).

ABOUT THE AUTHOR

KURT WILKIN is a gifted connector—of dots, ideas, and people.

For the past thirty years, he has advised high-growth companies, starting his career with Ernst & Young, and today in his roles as co-founder and visionary of HireBetter and managing partner of Bee Cave Capital. He is a serial entrepreneur with multiple successful exits and has helped hundreds of entrepreneurs and CEOs build their companies.

Kurt has called Texas, Louisiana, and Arkansas home his entire life and proudly claims to have "Redneck, Cajun, and Hillbilly rolled into one beautiful package." That might explain his natural BS detector. As you'll see in these pages, his plain-spoken, approachable style helps cut through the clutter and delivers lessons for fellow entrepreneurs that they can apply—right away.

He is the father of three active boys who don't let him take life too seriously, and he resides in Austin with his wife, Carrie, who didn't think he could focus long enough to get the grocery list right, much less write an entire book!